I Was a Hidden Child
"In the Name of God"

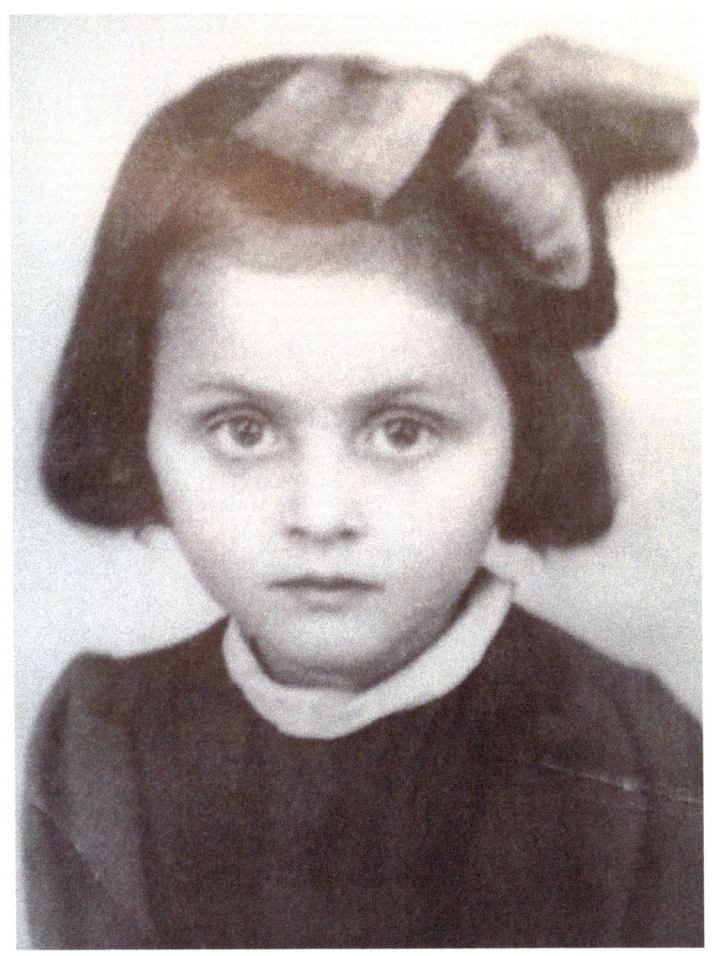

Miriam Ferber

Copyright © 2022 by the Ferber Foundation for Children

All rights reserved under International Copyright Conventions. No part of this book may be used or reproduced in any manner whatsoever without written permission from the publisher.

Printed in the United States of America

Kora Press ® is a federally registered trademark

ISBN: 978-0-9979047-9-6

Published by Kora Press ®
www.KoraPress.com

Mirosława and Stanisława Łączkowska, Sosnowiec, Poland, 1946

With my mother, Stanisława Łączkowska, 1947

With my mother, Stanisława Łączkowska, 1947

Ronny's Bar Mitzvah, with my mother Stanisława

CONTENTS

Preface.....Page 15

Chapter 1: Miriam.....Page 19
Hidden.....Page 24
Closure.....Page 29
Denounced.....Page 33
Scarlet Fever.....Page 34

Chaper 2: End of the War.....Page 37
The Rappaports.....Page 38
Uncles.....Page 40
Orphanage.....Page 42
Smuggled.....Page 44
Kidnapped.....Page 45
Bordrer Inspection.....Page 46
Jerzy Gryt.....Page 48
Courthouse.....Page 50
Kazimierz.....Page 52

Chapter 3: Identity Transitions.....Page 55
Baptism.....Page 56
Catholicism.....Page 57
School.....Page 59
Dating.....Page 67
Shadow of a Doubt.....Page 70
Moment of Truth.....Page 72
The Gypsy.....Page 73
Mrs. Cesarz.....Page 74
Mixed Feelings.....Page 77

Chapter 4: Leaving Poland.....Page 83
The Hirsches.....Page 84
A New Song.....Page 86

Belgium.....Page 87
My Mother's Fear.....Page 92
Becoming Stateless.....Page 94
Separated by Hirsch.....Page 95
Orphaned Again.....Page 95
The Grosses.....Page 99
Papa and Erna Freilich.....Page 102
Sława.....Page 105
"Be My Daughter".....Page 107
Goodbye Party.....Page 109

Chater 5: America.....Page 113
Lorraine and Cantor Shalom Nelson.....Page 114
New York.....Page 115
Harlem.....Page 116
Special Recording.....Page 118
Leah and Moishe Katz.....Page 118
Jewish Choices.....Page 119
Uncles and Aunt.....Page 121
Shabbat Invitations.....Page 124
Mrs. Lederman.....Page 126
Meeting Many Rabbis.....Page 129

Chapter 6: Finding Fred.....Page 131
The Right Decision.....Page 138
Papa and Erna Meet Fred.....Page 140
Rabbinical Blessings.....Page 142
Our Wedding.....Page 144
Homes.....Page 150
Friends.....Page 154
Wanda.....Page 157
Jurek.....Page 159
Giving.....Page 160
Recognizing Heroism.....Page 162
Finding Community.....Page 166

Visiting Poland.....Page 167
Dreaming of My Birth Parents.....Page 169
The Bracelet.....Page 170
Church and Wise Men.....Page 171
Yizkor.....Page 173
Final Communion.....Page 174

Family and Fiends' Album.....Page 180

Ronny's Bar Mitzvah, with my brother Jurek, my mother Stanisława and Fred, 1977

DEDICATION

Dedicated to the memory of my Catholic parents Stanisława and Józef Łączkowski. They risked their lives to save a Jewish child.

Dedicated to the many heroes who risked their lives to save others.

Wanda Łączkowska and Jurek Łączkowki, Sosnowiec, Poland, 1965
Honoring my Catholic sister and brother, Wanda and Jurek

Dedication

*Stanisława Łączkowska and Józef Łączkowski,
Sosnowiec, Poland, 1935
Honoring my Catholic father and mother.*

Ronny's Bar Mitzvah, my mother Stanisława, 1977

PREFACE

I was a child. The war had ended. I looked out the window of our attic apartment. Sunlight merged into the willow trees, the earth, and back toward the sky. The world was suddenly still.

People had disappeared. One could feel their absence. My own past was lost, as in a mist. I had been taught that Jesus was my friend. His image was in our home, in school, in church. But I felt as if all this didn't really belong to me.

As the years passed, I despaired of ever knowing who I was or would become. There was only my mom, our home, and vague memories that seemed like a dream. The intervening decades have unraveled much of my past, though not all. There is a deeper truth hiding beneath appearances.

I hope my journey will help you with yours, whether you are a Christian, a Jew, or of any other sect or religion. Beyond all our differences lies the vastness of our common humanity, awaiting our return.

Miriam Mączyk ~ Mirosława Łączkowska ~ Miriam Ferber

IN MEMORIAM

*Honoring the memory of my Jewish parents
Faygel and Shlomo Mączyk, and my brother Leo Mączyk, 1938*

Miriam and Fred, Acapulco, Mexico, 1969

WITH LOVE

Miriam and Fred, West Bloomfield, 1980

CHAPTER ONE
MIRIAM

I was born in Poland, in the city of Sosnowiec, but I don't know my exact birth date; although my birth certificate says May 26, 1942. All the members of my family—my mother, my father, and my brother—were murdered in the Holocaust. There is a story behind where my birth date came from, but first I think it's important to share some thoughts about my birth parents, and then about the family who raised me.

I was seven months old when my birth mother gave me up to rescue me from the mass murder of the Holocaust. I can summon up no memory of her, but I believe that somewhere within me, in my heart, in my soul, she has always been and will always be with me. Even in childhood I sensed her spirit, felt her absence, but could not explain or describe this inner presence.

In my life experience I have known only one mother—Stanisława Łączkowska—who risked her family, lost her husband, and suffered the forced exile of her daughter Wanda, all to save me. Beginning mostly after the war, when it was no longer an automatic death sentence to save a Jewish child from the Nazi Holocaust, the vague impression of a hidden past strengthened within me. I sensed that I'd had another life, almost dreamlike. The thoughts and feelings of a young child are beyond the reach of most adults. In children, the boundary between dream experience and waking experience is not so clear. These dreamlike feelings of a layered self, of an unclear past, were so strong that I can recall them today; I can recall the state-of-mind of my childhood.

My birth mother Faygel is elusive to me. I cannot say when it was that I first had an inkling, or an intuition, that I had two identities. The dreamlike sense of another identity strengthened slowly. Others sensed it as well, especially as I reached adolescence. Sometimes children would tease me about being different, about being Jewish. Neither my childhood friends nor I had a clear idea what it meant to be Jewish. We just knew that it was dangerous, or wrong. Of course, rumors have lives of their own and rumors from the lips of children haunted me, just as vague impressions of a dream mother haunted me from within. That's the only way I can try to explain my feelings in those early years.

Now, of course, I fully realize how profoundly my birth mother Faygel sacrificed herself, how she suffered, giving away her daughter, holding onto her son, knowing it was the only possible hope of saving either of us. It was a time of world war and turmoil impossible to describe or imagine if we had not experienced it. Few knew what was really underway—the magnitude of the genocidal war against the Jews, and the scope of the murder.

The angel who took me as her own, Stanisława, was

My uncle and my father: Yisrael Mączyk (left), Shlomo Mączyk (right), 1935

throughout my life and up until her death the only mother I ever knew. And so, mourning the loss of my mother not just once, but twice, has also been a reality for me. I harbor a sensation of guilt for not feeling closer to the birth mother whose existence to me is like a distant photo from a distant past.

My birth mother's maiden name was Faygel Zeilender. Her Hebrew name was Tzipporah. My firstborn child is named after her. My mother was the only child of a prominent, *balbattish* (quiet, respectable) family. Her father had a well-known kosher butcher shop in Chorzów, Poland, a southern city near Katowice occupied by the Nazis in September of 1939. My mother was known for her beauty, and I have pictures that show it's true.

My father was Shlomo Mączyk, a tailor. Before my parents met, my mother was close friends with Yisrael Mączyk, my father's brother, and it was Yisrael who made the match between my parents. My father Shlomo and uncle Yisrael had a small tailor shop together. They had a sister, Hanka, as well as other sisters and brothers. My parents were religious Jews. My husband Freddy's mother, Rose Ferber, actually knew my mother when she was in her teens.

My uncle (middle left), and father Shlomo Mączyk (middle right) and their siblings, 1935

I Was a Hidden Child

Rose admired Faygel because during the holy Yom Kippur prayers she would stand all day, never sitting even once. One must be devoted and pious to stand all day while fasting.

I'm sure my parents had some schooling. I know they spoke Polish and Yiddish. People focused more on their vocations at that time; they were not college graduates. I do know they went to Heder, the Jewish afternoon school, for their Jewish education.

My parents' first child was my brother, Leo Mączyk, who was born in Chorzów in 1937. When the Nazis occupied Poland in September 1939, all Jews were told to leave Chorzów and its surrounding areas because these were reclaimed by Nazi Germany and reserved for *Volksdeutsche*—people of German origin or sympathy—and considered German territory, as it had been before World War I. Jews from Chorzów were moved to Sosnowiec and placed under a Jewish Council.

In Sosnowiec, my mother, father, and brother lived in a

My mother Faygel (center) with two friends on either side and my brother Leo Mączyk in the bugggy, Poland, 1938

Faygel Mączyk and Leo Mączyk, Poland, 1938

beautiful three-story apartment building. Across the street was a quiet park full of weeping willows. In my home I have a painting of the building that makes it look like a dream. The building was probably over a hundred years old when we moved in. Today the building is a landmark of Sosnowiec because of its beauty.

The apartment building was rectangular and built around a courtyard. As you entered the building and walked into the foyer, there were two sets of stairs. To the right, a staircase serviced half of the building, and to the left was a staircase for the other half. If you walked straight, you came to a door to the courtyard. My family moved into an apartment on the middle floor, on the left side of the building. Though the building remains, sadly the park and the willow trees are no more. Apartments were built in their place.

When we moved into our apartment, about sixty families lived there. Originally, the entire building was rented to Jewish people, but later, when they fled, gentiles moved into their apartments. My father befriended our Polish neighbors, the Łączkowskis. Stanisława and Józef Łączkowski were middle-aged and their two children, Wanda and Jurek, were 17 and 18 years old.

In America, neighbors are often outgoing and friendly, but during the war people in Poland were more cautious when letting strangers into their lives. Stanisława was shy and reserved. She was more of a loner and not one to mix with others. Józef was an outgoing guy and I was told that he and my father spent a lot of time together.

The Łączkowskis lived on the third floor in the middle apartment that faced the street. They had three large rooms with ceilings that were lower than the rest of the apartments. Even though the building was beautiful on the outside, the apartment was primitive. It was really an attic, like the Anne Frank house in Amsterdam. There was no running water in our apartment, and we shared a common bathroom with our neighbors. They chose this building because it was what they could afford. Józef was a plumber and didn't have steady work. When war broke out in 1939, they didn't feel the need to take over one of the newly vacant Jewish apartments, which they could have done.

HIDDEN

In 1942, sometime in November or December, as I was told, my family, along with the entire Jewish population of Sosnowiec was taken to the Środula Ghetto, a remnant ghetto in a suburb of Sosnowiec.

The house Miriam lived in, Piłsudskiego 42, m. 10, Sosnowiec

I Was a Hidden Child

My courtyard, my playground, Sosnowiec, Poland

When we were taken to the ghetto, Józef said to Stanisława, "You know what? The Mączyk family has been taken to the ghetto. They are going to keep their son with them, but they'd like to leave their little girl with us." Stanisława did not hesitate. She wholeheartedly agreed to take me in. There really was no time for planning. Józef had talked it over with my parents and Stanisława knew about those discussions, but the friendship was between the two men.

I don't think the Łączkowskis could have imagined what they were getting into. Perhaps they thought it would be like babysitting a seven-month-old child for a while, until her parents could return. No one envisioned the horrors of Nazism.

This Polish couple had to go into the Środula Ghetto and get me out, putting their lives at risk. There was a curfew. Jews could not leave the ghetto whenever they wanted to, certainly not with a child. The night before my rescue, my Jewish father somehow brought

Miriam

Jurek Łączkowski, Stanisława Łączkowska, Jozef Łączkowski, Wanda Łączkowska, Poland, 1933

Stanisława a Star of David armband which she tucked into her purse. The next morning, Stanisława, this righteous gentile woman, soon to be my mother, put on the Star of David and walked into the ghetto. My mother handed me over to her in a buggy. Stanisława Łączkowska arrived alone but left with an infant, with me.

Józef and their son Jurek were waiting for us at the ghetto gate. Stanisława removed the Star of David. She had walked into the ghetto a Jew with a Star of David armband and walked out a gentile with no armband. That is how they brought me into their home. They called me Mirosława, or Mira for short.

Stanisława didn't ask my mother about my birth date. I believe she never imagined my mother, father, and brother would perish in a concentration camp. She knew only that I was seven months old. My parents kept my brother Leo with them because it was hard to find a place for a five-year-old who spoke already, and there was no hiding a circumcision. It was more difficult for a boy to be saved during the war than a girl. Also, my birth mother just didn't want to

Jozef Łączkowski, Sosnowiec, Poland, circa 1938

part with Leo. But both of my parents thought it would be safer for a seven-month-old girl to stay with another family.

There was no getting around that stark reality that the ghetto was the ghetto. My parents and Leo were transferred to Auschwitz about three months later. As an adult I learned from people who had somehow survived Auschwitz that my family had been exterminated together in a gas chamber. This unimaginable black hole in my life does not diminish with time.

CLOSURE

Much later I discovered that my birth mother was able to come visit

Stanisława Łączkowska, Sosnowiec, 1947

me one time before the ghetto was liquidated. It was only a few days after she had given me to Stanisława. She missed me so much that she had to visit me, to see me, to hold me again. Some Jews were allowed to go out of the ghetto before the curfew, but I don't know how my mother did it. She may have been smuggled out. During the visit my mother held me close in her arms and expressed her gratitude to this Polish family, Stanisława and Józef, for opening their hearts to me. That day was the last time my birth mother ever saw or held me. That was the end. I don't believe she could have realized that it was. Surely, she thought she was there for a visit and would see me again soon.

My mother left and never had the chance to come back. My Polish mother Stanisława spoke to me often of that last meeting. The experience was powerful for her and seemed to mark the turning point in her becoming my mother for the next 19 years and more.

In later years, after I had discovered that I was Jewish, Stanisława described the way my birth mother had held me close and cuddled me. When my birth mother Faygel left, my Polish mother Stanisława watched her through the apartment window. Stanisława gazed out the window and watched my birth mother walk across the street, into the park. This park, no longer there, was filled with weeping willow trees. My birth mother jumped slightly to grasp one of the branches overhead. Stanisława felt this was a sign that my birth mother was at peace now, though sad, but at peace, relieved in knowing that I was now safe in a loving home. Stanisława also sought closure, so this is how she explained my mother's little jump to grasp a weeping willow branch, on her way back to the grim reality of the ghetto.

My mother was about 26 years old that last time she saw me. She had left me and I believe she was at peace. Although during my birth mother's visit Stanisława hadn't thought to ask her my birth date, she later calculated a birth date for me. The visit was in December. Because Stanisława knew I was seven months old, she just counted back seven months: November, October, September, August, July, June, May. And since her own birthday was April 26, she

decided that my birthday would also be the 26th. May 26th, 1942—
that's what is on my birth certificate. This was the beginning of my
life as a member of the Łączkowski family.

Wanda Łączkowska, my Polish sister

Stanisława and Józef became my parents in every way that I knew.
Wanda and Jurek became my sister and brother. From that moment
on, the Łączkowskis became my Polish family. I was with them from
the age of seven months. I called Stanisława and Józef, "*Mamusia*"
and "*Tatuś*," Mommy and Daddy. We were in every way a family; though war raged all around us, we lived very happily for three
years. We were fortunate to be sheltered from the worst, that is, until
that day—the day we were denounced.

The Łączkowski family quite rightfully could have moved into my parents' apartment, which was larger and on a lower floor, now that the apartment was empty and I was a part of their family. But Józef and Stanisława did not move. Stanisława said that she preferred the attic apartment. She actually loved her attic home and ended up living there for fifty years.

The apartment had wooden floors that I scrubbed on my

My sister Wanda and her husband, my brother-in-law, Janusz, Poland 1943

hands and knees. Either because of the drudgery, or maybe the connection with painful memories, I just could never bring myself to scrub floors any more in later years. Scrubbing floors had become anathema to me. At the time, I just accepted this chore as natural. But later, the task brought on bad feelings.

Life was peaceful in those years, despite the war that raged around us. We felt as if we lived in the eye of the storm. The war crashed down upon us only near the very end. Most particularly, on the day we were denounced. That day, our lives turned upside down and we were suddenly caught in a storm, rather than sheltered in the storm's eye.

DENOUNCED

The betrayal came late in the war. We were seemingly moments away from escaping the Nazi terrors. But then, suddenly and viciously, we were betrayed just three months before war's end. In another ninety days or so, the Russians liberated the city.

The apartment building's janitor was possibly rewarded for turning us over to the Nazi SS. Or maybe her motive was just pure hatred. She did not like the fact that the quiet middle-aged Polish Catholic Łączkowski couple had a little baby. My mother Stanisława was 40 years old. My father Józef was 44. The caretaker asked questions, created a stir, and finally went directly to the SS, the *Schutzstaffel* protective squadron—an elite Nazi unit. She must have insinuated that there was a Jewish child in this family and also that the family listened to a shortwave radio. Listening to the news on a shortwave radio was strictly forbidden. The Germans searched our apartment and found the shortwave radio and headphones.

The SS came in the middle of the night. They arrested my father Józef, Stanisława, and me. They took us to jail in Sosnowiec. Stanisława and Józef, having anticipated their possible arrest, had planned their stories to make sure they matched. They agreed to tell everyone that I was most certainly not a Jewish child. No! I was, in fact, the illegitimate child of their runaway daughter, Wanda.

Because of their cover story, Wanda was compelled to disappear, to run away. Stanisława believed that if the Germans had found Wanda they would have somehow checked her blood against my blood and they would have discovered that I was not Wanda's daughter and our entire family would have been killed by the Nazis.

In the Sosnowiec jail, Józef was placed in one cell while Stanisława and I were locked in another, separated by a wall. I remember looking through a little peephole between the cells. The Germans interrogated us and held us there for an entire month. Today this memory feels almost like a dream, but I have a distinct memory of seeing my father Józef in jail. I looked through the peephole and saw him pacing back and forth. I also remember, as in a dream, the women who sat with me and my mother in the cell. They were very nice to me. I remember walking around the German soldiers and touching their guns, even sitting on their laps. They spoke German to me, perhaps thinking that if I knew Yiddish I would respond. Maybe I was kind of entertaining to them. My mother said she was afraid that maybe they would get mad, but I was just a cute kid, and they took pity on me. My Polish mother Stanisława was very smart, very strong, and she loved very deeply. She was like a tigress guarding her family. She fought with the Nazis and demanded, "Why are you arresting us? This is my granddaughter. My daughter had an illegitimate child. She ran away and left her with me." The Germans eventually believed her story and finally released us. They were supposed to release my father, too, but didn't, perhaps because they had found the shortwave radio. There were many political prisoners at that time.

SCARLET FEVER

Sometime in 1945, maybe a week or so after we were detained for that month, I came down with scarlet fever. This was before Józef was taken by the Germans to Mauthausen Concentration Camp in Austria.

People couldn't just walk in the streets because a curfew was in effect, not only for Jewish people but for everybody. But I was very sick and was having a hard time breathing. I was suffocating. Stanisława knew a Polish doctor whose home was nearby. At around two in the morning, in defiance of the curfew, she just walked to his house and knocked on his door. The doctor said he would not come and asked her to wait until the curfew was over at seven in the morning. Stanisława wouldn't take no for an answer. She went to a few more doctors that night but they all told her the same thing, "We'll come, but only after the curfew."

Stanisława had heard about a female doctor within walking distance and thought, "Oh, a female doctor will have more compassion and will probably come." So she went to this doctor's elaborate building, saw a guard standing in front of a huge iron door. After speaking to him, my mother was led to the doctor's apartment and told the doctor, "My child cannot breathe." But the doctor said that she absolutely would not violate the curfew for fear of being killed. This was my mother's last resort and she left crying.

As she was going down the stairs, the building guard was standing by the huge iron door and asked my mother why she was crying. Stanisława told him, "My last hope of finding a doctor was this lady. I thought she would have compassion for my child for she is a mother herself." The caretaker looked at her and said, "That woman? She wouldn't help you because she's a goddamn Jew." When my mother Stanisława heard this, she made a U-turn. She went back to the doctor's door and knocked. The doctor said, "I told you that I will not go with you. I will come to your apartment after the curfew." My mother looked at her and whispered, "I have a Jewish child in my house. I am jeopardizing my life and my family's life. You must come with me and help me." The doctor was scared, but she quickly agreed, "Okay, but you have to bring me back." My mother assured her, "Yes. I will bring you back."

They walked to our apartment, and the doctor treated me to help me breathe. Then, as she had promised, my mother walked the doctor back home. Stanisława had endangered herself, her family, and the doctor in order to save my life. At seven in the morning, after the curfew ended, the other doctors she'd visited in the middle of the night did start coming, but I was already much better.

My mother was always the tigress; she overcame the fear of capture and death to save me. Luckily the doctor was Jewish, and luckily the caretaker had an anti-Semitic outburst. It was not a coincidence. It was *bashert*; it was destined, it was meant to be.

Every time my mother revealed that I was Jewish, she was putting herself at risk. She had to make choices about who could be trusted and who not. My mother was always guarded but she knew in this case that it would be safe since the doctor was Jewish and putting her own life in jeopardy as much as my mother's.

CHAPTER TWO
END OF THE WAR

For a while Józef remained in prison in Sosnowiec, but then the Germans deported him. When Józef was walking to the train station for deportation, he wrote a letter and he dropped it on the street, hoping it would reach Stanisława. Sure enough, someone brought it to my mother. He wrote that they were sending him somewhere, to one of the concentration camps. He was sent to Mauthausen Concentration Camp.

One of Józef's sisters who lived close to the German border had become a supporter of Nazi Germany. She went to parties for German soldiers and became part of everything that was German. Stanisława used to call her a *Volksdeutsch*, an ethnic German, though Stanisława used the term loosely. She felt her sister-in-law was a Nazi sympathizer. This reminds me of the movie *Gloomy Sunday* that shows how people would give the Germans special treatment thinking that it would help them later. When my father Józef was in Mauthausen, Stanisława went to this sister of Józef and told her, "Your brother has been arrested. Maybe you can do something." Her answer to my mother was "Well, that's the way he made his bed, let him sleep in it." Despite the fact that my mother begged, my father's sister refused to lift a finger to help. My mother never again said a friendly word to her sister-in-law.

My Polish father died in Mauthausen just a week or two before the war ended. We found out that he had died of typhoid fever because after the war a neighbor of ours who had shared a cell with him came to tell my mother how he had died.

After the war, though my mother and I could have moved to a larger apartment, we stayed in the attic apartment, just the two of us. Jurek was someplace in Germany. They sent him there for hard labor; I never found out exactly where. But he came back. And so did Wanda.

Ever since we had been turned in to the SS, everything had changed. All the neighbors sensed or suspected that the child living with Stanisława was Jewish. They discussed it among themselves; gossiping I suppose you might say. I had no idea, and Stanisława said nothing about it to me. But it caught up to me later in my childhood when some children started to call me "Żydówa, Żydówa," a word that means "Jewess" but that is used more like "kike." Sometimes, someone might call me "Żydóweczka," a term of endearment they used sarcastically to mock me. Some even schemed about what they could do to me, but none followed through, probably out of fear of the post-war Communist regime.

For almost 19 years my mother lived in fear that my Jewish origins would bring anti-Semitic persecution. The remarks the Poles made were appalling, hateful. But she had an even more personal and more fundamental fear. She feared that I might leave her. She had a realistic sense of the future and recognized that there was no future for me as a Jew in Poland. Of course, she was right and eventually I did leave.

THE RAPPAPORTS

For a while during the war, my Polish mother Stanisława hid a Jewish family, the Rappaports, in our attic apartment. They were a husband and wife who came and asked to spend the night. They didn't want to leave. The situation was similar to Anne Frank's because our attic had a room hidden by a large bookshelf, and no one knew there was a door behind it. But though I was there at the same time, I cannot remember the Rappaports, probably because my mother kept them hidden. They were there for maybe two or three weeks. My mother hid them, fed them, gave them all that we had to give. But then one night, without saying goodbye, really without a word, they just went away. The Rappaports just vanished from our lives.

End of the War

Stanisława often wondered why they never contacted her again. I

The door to a hidden room in our attic where Stanisława hid the Rappaport family

kept saying, "*Mamusia*, maybe they got killed."

I am sure Stanisława would have let them stay longer at our apartment. Why they left without a word, where they went, and why they never communicated with us again I'll never know. Even after the war, everything was hush hush, "*sha shtill*," so we never talked about the Rappaports. There were so many taboo subjects because of the Communist regime. People talked quietly and lived in constant fear. They feared discussing wartime memories of any kind. The act of helping Jewish people during the war was no longer a crime in post-war Poland, but fear and habits of secrecy were not cast aside under the Communist regime. Though no one was honored for helping Jews, no one was harmed either.

Today, there is a chief rabbi of Poland and an Israeli ambassador. Righteous Christians have been honored. Poland is a democratic country with freedom of speech and of religion.

UNCLES

In 1945, a few months after the war, two men showed up at our door, unannounced, unexpected. One claimed to be my Uncle Jacob, brother of my birth father Shlomo.

How did they know where to look for me? My uncle Yisrael had been close to my birth mother. He and my birth father had owned a tailoring shop in Chorzów. Amazingly, he had received a letter from my birth mother sometime during the war. Yisrael had been in Auschwitz. The letter from her came to him hidden in the collar of someone's shirt. So he knew where I was the whole time. My birth mother's note said, "I am leaving Miriam at the Łączkowskis, and this is the address."

Of course, my Polish mother wouldn't allow me to go with them. She said to my uncle Yisrael, "Look, it's only a few months after the war. I don't know, maybe her mother will come for her. Or maybe you can come back in a few months. But I am not giving you the child now." So they said thank you and goodbye and they never came back. I confirmed later that it had been my uncle Jack (Yisrael)

End of the War

Mirosława and Stanisława Łączkowska, Sosnowiec, 1954

and his friend Motek. From this time on, Stanisława remained for me my mother. She is the only mother I have ever known in my conscious memory. We lived alone, just the two of us. We counted our pennies, and often buying food was an ordeal. We had no help from anyone. In order to take care of me, Stanisława had to take in work at home where she sewed industrial gloves as a freelancer. She'd walk to the factory and pick up the very stiff pre-cut industrial gloves, ready to sew, and after stitching them together, she and I would turn them right side out, since they were sewn inside out. I felt that I really helped her and it was hard work. She had to do this work at home so I wouldn't be left alone. We also boarded a few students to bring in extra income.

ORPHANAGE

It was 1946, one year after the war. Józef had died in Mauthausen Concentration Camp, Jurek was a student in Kraków, and Wanda was married. My mother and I lived alone, just the two of us. She continued to sew gloves for factory workers. Because I was only four-years-old, I was too young and Stanisława could not send me to kindergarten. These were the toughest times for us.

One day there was another surprise unannounced knock on the door. A woman came in and said to my mother, "Look, Mrs. Łączkowska, we know that you have a Jewish child. We have an orphanage in Bytom, and we would love to help you."

This woman was not the head of the orphanage, but she was in charge of finding and fetching Jewish children who had been orphaned in the war. I must have been registered in the Jewish *Gmina* (Polish: Community Center), or maybe the neighbor had said something. But she somehow found out that I was at Mrs. Łączkowska's.

My mother often recalled details of the woman's visit. Her name was Mrs. Lederman. She knew how to persuade my mother and told her, "We know that you're a widow and that it must be difficult finding work while Mirusia is at home. She's too young for kindergarten, and too old for nursery school, so please let us help you. We would love to help out until you get settled with a regular job. We will keep Mirusia all week long, but you can come any time to visit her, especially at the weekends. The door will always be open for you."

End of the War

She handed my mother $100 in US dollars and said, "I want you to take this money. Maybe you can exchange it for złotys to make your life a little bit easier while you look for work. I guarantee that Mirusia will be very well cared for and you will be relieved."

My mother thought this woman was a good person who was trying to help her. After much discussion with Jurek and Wanda, my brother and sister, Stanisława accepted the offer. Oh, what wonderful people, she thought. It was financially a welcome relief. The offer had come at a good time.

But the hundred dollars sat in a drawer. My mother never used them. When I got older, my mother would sometimes show me the money and say, "This is for your dowry, for your future, when you get married." When she showed it to me, I didn't know where it had come from. Much later, I asked my mother if my family had left any money or valuables. "No. They didn't leave anything for you," she said, "they always thought they were coming back, that they would see you again."

I recall that the principal of the orphanage had a beard. I didn't know he was a Jew, let alone an observant Jew, and he looked odd to me. The food there was also different, sometimes odd to me. It was kosher, though I had no idea what that might mean. I couldn't have the *kiełbasa* (sausage) I liked, not that I'd had much of it anyway since we could barely afford it.

Also odd to me was that I didn't see any crosses on the wall or pictures of the Holy Mother or Jesus. But every night before going to bed I knelt to pray. The orphanage staff tolerated this Polish Catholic little girl's prayers for a while, but after some weeks it became a problem. I couldn't understand why, but after a few weeks they told me not to kneel any more. They'd just say, "Don't do that." But even though they were religious Jews, they never pressured me to say any particular prayers such as the *Shema Yisrael* (Deuteronomy 6:4–8. "Hear, O Israel, the Lord is our God, the Lord is One.")

SMUGGLED

My mother came to visit me often, but over time, Stanisława began to suspect something. She felt the people running the orphanage were not eager for her to visit. After a few weeks, my mother felt they were actually trying to keep her away. She originally thought the orphanage was helping her out so she could go to work, but after a month of this, she started to have mixed feelings and a change of heart.

Then, one night, my mother had a terrible dream. There was cement, a whole yard of cement. And she started to walk on it. All of a sudden her husband Józef came out of the cement and asked her, "What have you done? Why did you take Mirusia to that place?" My mother was shaken by this dream, but she never told me about it. She would have been ashamed to tell me. Instead, I learned of it from a very good friend of my mother's who had also hidden a Jewish girl. This woman let her daughter go in 1956 when she found family in Israel.

My mother told me that she had tried once or twice to remove me from the orphanage. I remember one of those times. She asked the maid to find me upstairs and told her to say, "Your mommy's waiting." Instead of coming down, I started screaming, "Mommy, Mommy, Mommy!" and the plan fell through. The housekeeper got in trouble. I found out later that they almost fired her. Perhaps it was the cement dream that inspired such heroic efforts from my mother.

Finally, my mother came to the orphanage one day and said, "I miss my daughter too much. I cannot do this. I cannot just come here for the weekends. I need her back home. Thank you for your help." And the head of the orphanage said to her, "You know what? You are absolutely right. Why don't you come after the weekend? We will prepare her for you and pack her up. Why don't you come on, say, Tuesday, to pick her up?"

And when my mother came to get me on Tuesday, I was not there. They had taken me from my mother with motives they felt were pure. They had acted "in the name of God!"

Two days before my mother came to get me, they'd embarked on a plan to smuggle me out of Poland and send me to Israel. Their logic was that they did this in the name of God. I say, "in the name of God" today, looking back. But I was only four years old, having no idea that I was in a Jewish orphanage or that I was Jewish. All I felt was that I was being thrown out of the orphanage and sent away. Though my mother knew it was a Jewish organization, she had no inkling they took us into this "orphanage" in order to send us to Israel. In the name of God. They simply didn't want Jewish children being raised by non-Jews.

I had gotten more comfortable with the principal of the orphanage by then. I had friends at the orphanage, and I felt safe there. Suddenly my life there came to an abrupt and terrifying end. I remember vividly the day the principal handed me over to a total stranger, a stranger I'd never seen before. I was sent out into the world, a world unknown to me, and off on a train trip with a stranger. No one ever tried to explain to me what was happening. They never told me where I was going. No one told me what to expect in a way that a four-year-old might understand. The strange man, my chaperone, gave me some candies, but never explained anything to me.

I cried. I shivered from the cold and from fear. I vividly remember the train, the loud noises, the banging metallic sounds and the hissing steam. And I remember the train starting out, going very slowly. But most of all, I remember my fear, and my tears. Soon I became hysterical. Unbeknownst to me, I was being transported to a new land, a new life, a new orphanage perhaps, and all "in the name of God."

KIDNAPPED

These people did a lot in the name of God. I feel today that this was kidnapping. They never took into consideration all that my Polish mother Stanisława had done for me. She had jeopardized her own life, her family's lives, sacrificed her daughter Wanda's reputation, and lost her husband—all to protect me.

I deeply respect all religions, certainly Judaism, and in that sense, I understand their motivation, in the name of God. But to me, these people were unquestionably cruel. They simply wanted Jewish children out of Polish homes, at all costs, and they showed up wherever they heard about hidden children. I discovered later that they didn't care or understand how these righteous and caring Polish people had jeopardized their very lives to save Jewish children, perhaps also in the name of God. No. They just took the children away and sent them off to be Jews in Israel.

I've experienced similar attitudes and ideas even today in certain Jewish communities. But I've learned we must be careful with our ideas of what constitutes Jewish knowledge. It's easy enough to invent a reality based on a narrow foundation of knowledge. And so, it's easy to become extreme. This mentality of absolute knowledge is used by cults but should never be an aspect of Judaism, for Judaism is of course not a cult.

Although I am grateful for how my life turned out, I still feel how painful, hurtful it was to separate me from my mother. My life was not in jeopardy. I was loved. I was comfortable. I was raised as a Christian and not tricked into a cult. Maybe I didn't have luxuries others enjoyed, but I was certainly not suffering or malnourished.

BORDER INSPECTION

On the border of Czechoslovakia, at Zebrzydowice, the train carrying me and my chaperone stopped. All the passengers had to get out and wait on the platform for a border inspection. It took hours and hours and hours. I fell asleep at the station while waiting. The security guards were going through the luggage at the train station and were looking for dollars, I think.

At about four or five in the morning, I woke up and saw a most frightening sight—a Jewish man praying with his prayer shawl and *phylacteries* (head and arm amulets with straps), *tallis* and *tefillin*. He seemed to me an apparition, a ghost. For a four-year-old child, it was traumatic. Seeing this ghost, I became terrified and I started crying hysterically. My wailing attracted attention.

Everyone was searched by a UB (Polish: UB is short for *Urząd Bezpieczeństwa,* the Soviet-controlled internal security police

Jerzy Gryt and Mira, Sosnowiec, 1979

in Poland, established in 1944) inspector, and my sobbing brought scrutiny upon us. The man I was traveling with had about $35 in his sock and the Security Police found it. My chaperone was a young man, this stranger who had carried me off without explanation or preparation. He was maybe 30-years-old, though to me he looked old. He was smuggling money for himself for his journey to Israel. American money had power, but in Communist Poland it was a crime to have dollars. You could have *bony*, sort of like a traveler's check, though it didn't work like cash. But this man had real American dollars.

When they took his money, my chaperone became totally unhinged and he started crying alongside me. Now there were two of us crying aloud. He told the inspector that it was the only money he had. Making matters even worse, I began crying louder and pleading for my mommy, "I want my mommy, *mamusi, mamusi!*" The inspector demanded from my chaperone, "What's going on here?" And then my chaperone started to talk.

"You took this $35 from me, and now I have this child. I don't even know who she is. They sent me with her." No one ever asked my chaperone who I was—he just volunteered the information. I kept crying out, "*Do mamusi, do mamusi*" (Polish: "To my mother, to my mother"). He was of course terrified by now.

JERZY GRYT

The UB inspector was only 25 or 26 years old. I remember that he was tall and handsome. The UB inspector looked at my passport and saw that the picture and the stamp did not match. There was something wrong and a frantic scene unfolded on the station platform with me, the chaperone, and the inspector.

I was shivering as well as sobbing. It was cold and I had no coat. The UB inspector separated me from the chaperone and allowed him to go. He had wrapped me in his jacket. My shivering had stopped but I was as lost as ever, and he took me to his house in Katowice, which was at least thirty miles away. I could not fully understand then that he was saving me, but he was. Amidst all the turmoil of war and post-war, he reached out to a child in need and did not abandon her.

We traveled to his home in an open truck. I stayed with him and his wife, Jerzy and Magdalena Gryt. They were newlyweds, and Magdalena was pregnant with twins. Now I was all alone in the world except for this couple. They let me sleep between them. It was an overwhelming experience for me as a four-year-old. Slowly my fear subsided and I began to feel safe with them, and warm. But when I woke the next morning, I felt as alone and lost as ever.

I cried and cried. They did their best to calm me. I described

Mira and Jerzy Gryt, Sosnowiec, 1992

my mother, "*Mamusia's* name is Stanisława Łączkowska. She wears a cross. She lives in our town, Sosnowiec. Oh! I don't know my address. On one side of our house there is a butcher shop. There is a patisserie next door, on the other side. I can see the willow trees from the window." And on and on. My savior, Jerzy Gryt, held a high position in the UB, so he called his colleagues and told them, "Listen! Go to the city of Sosnowiec and find me this mother whose child we are sheltering." When they returned without results, he sent them back. The quest went on. He simply wouldn't take no for an answer.

Jerzy Gryt had become my angel, my guardian. After a week of searching, they found my mother. She left Sosnowiec immediately and came to pick me up. When Stanisława arrived, I cried tears of joy and relief even more abundant than the tears of fear and loneliness which had attracted Jerzy's attention on that fateful night at the train station. Jerzy and Magdalena became our lifelong friends, and that's how I know this story today. Jerzy said he'd always remember the way my mother and I kissed and hugged when we were reunited. Later, Jerzy got out of the UB. He was a truly righteous man, and I stayed in touch with Jerzy and Magdalena until they both passed on.

Being suddenly and terrifyingly uprooted from a safe daily routine and sent off with a strange man on a train trip felt more like a dream memory than an actual memory. What was real and what was terrifying or imaginary to me as a four-year-old merged into a singular traumatic recollection. My mother and the Gryts recounted to me my seeming kidnapping and rescue when I was able to better understand. But I experienced it all as a nightmare. I'm telling you, traumatic events can cause memory blackouts. For many years I thought it had not actually occurred other than as a nightmare or a dreamlike imagination.

COURTHOUSE

Doomed from the start, akin to a kidnapping at the hands of an unknown man, that first attempt to smuggle me off to Israel ended in tragic and comic failure. My mother Stanisława retrieved me from my rescuers, the Gryts, ending that first kidnapping. Not content with the first fiasco and terrifying kidnapping, the Jewish organization in Poland tried to get me once again when I was seven years old. They took my circumstances to the Polish legal system, brought my mother to court, and told them that I was not her child. These Jewish "missionaries" said I was Jewish, and they wanted to take me based upon my religion, irrespective of the circumstances of my rescue by Stanisława and her family, irrespective of my life with her, my mother. The judge was doubtless shocked to see a little seven-year-old girl screaming uncontrollably, again, "*Mamusia, mamusia,*" pleading to be allowed to stay with her mommy, sobbing as she clutched desperately her mother's leg for safety.

Having witnessed sufficient drama to convince him, the judge became frustrated and probably overwhelmed by the scene and made his decision on the spot. He spoke sternly to the representative of the Jewish organization, "You know what? Enough, enough! When she is 18 years old, then, and not before, she and she alone will decide where to go. Until then, just leave her alone. That is the court's order. Settled!" This pronouncement by the judge, allowing me to stay with *mamusia*, was like a stay of execution, a pardon. I felt certain I was not Jewish and I remember the emotion, the sense of escape from a cruel fate that had been planned for me.

As a result of this near escape, I became afraid of policemen or anyone in a uniform. I became terrified that at any moment someone would snatch me up and carry me away from my mother. Now I know that we went to court, fighting my removal from our home, a few times. These traumatic experiences melded into a singular traumatic memory, and this memory comes to me as if it were a bad dream. Stanisława was also afraid and always on edge because she knew the Jewish community was trying to get me. Later on, I put two and two together because my mother explained to me what was happening. I remember clearly the courthouse building, as if from a nightmare, but still distinct. I've shown it to Fred, my husband, on one of our visits to Poland and it is now a landmark.

KAZIMIERZ

My sister Wanda got married in 1945, right after the war. Her husband Janusz was a kind and good man. He was a coal mining engineer and held a high position. Whenever there was a fire in a mine, he was concerned only about the miners who worked for him. He would always rush to be there, and they loved him for it. My sister and he settled in Kazimierz.

Wanda and Janusz had a beautiful house with a garden, and my mother and I often visited them. It was like an open house where they held wonderful parties. They had a car, a telephone, and two baby grand pianos which was most unusual for Poles in 1953. Janusz played guitar and piano and he sang beautifully. I often sang along with him. They had two daughters and a son. The first child was Basia (born 1945, shortly after they had married), then Hania (born 1947), and then Jacek (born 1953).

They lived in a beautiful upscale area. My mother and I spent almost every weekend there and enjoyed many parties and family gatherings. The garden was filled with wonderful apple trees, plum trees, raspberries, gooseberries, and other fruits.

These were beautiful and peaceful times for us. My sister Wanda was warm, thoughtful, and loving. They could afford certain luxuries. So often we stayed there for an entire weekend, relaxed, and ate wonderful foods. Whatever instrument Janusz touched, the music he created seemed miraculous.

Wanda and Janusz were a central experience in my life growing up and my heart warms to remember the beautiful parties, the holy suppers before Christmas, the elaborate food, the special preparations and festivities for New Year's Eve and Day. Wanda was 17 or 18 years older than I so she was more like a second mother to me than a sister. According to Stanisława's cover story, Wanda had been the "runaway mother" who had "abandoned" me. She had been brave and loved me enough to really run away to protect me in case the Germans had actually compared our blood and discovered that she wasn't really my mother.

Wanda, when she did have her own children, was really the ideal image of a mother. Her three children were not that much younger than I was. Basia, Hania, and Jacek were my friends. Even though they were younger, we were almost contemporaries. I had wonderful times with them.

Miriam Ferber's time to sing, at her home, 2019

CHAPTER THREE
IDENTITY TRANSITIONS

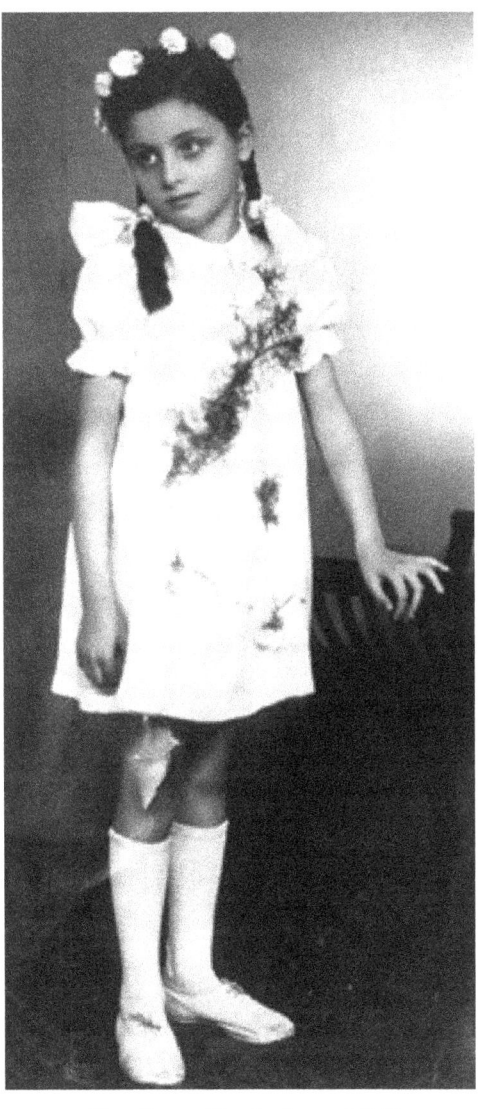

When I was seven-years-old, it was time to enroll in school. The Catholic Church was of course dominant in Poland, so I actually needed a certificate of baptism to enroll. Most importantly, my mother felt a strong responsibility to create a paper trail showing that I was Catholic. My mother could see into the future and knew that if there were clues, even a school record, that might make me appear to be Jewish, my identity could be exposed. Had she registered me as a Jew, she would no doubt have been approached by Jewish relief organizations offering "assistance." She also would have subjected me to a lifetime of problems from the neighbors.

Baptism, Kazimierz, 1949

I Was a Hidden Child

First communion, Sosnowiec, 1951

BAPTISM

Later on, my mother got the idea that the church in Kazimierz would baptize me. It was a suburb, and no one would know about it. But Kazimierz was a small town and people there wondered about me. Rumors started. The residents of Kazimierz knew something was not right. Why did a seven-year-old need to be baptized when baptism always took place at the age of one or two months? Stanisława persisted. It was the right thing to do.

I remember every detail of being baptized. I had no shoes to wear to the baptism. So you know what I did? I took sneakers and painted them with white chalk. I wore a very simple dress and the sneakers. Every time I touched something, the chalk came off. I loved my dress. My mother decorated the dress with greenery and fresh flowers. In my baptism picture I see a Jewish face with a cross. But the priest had the courage to baptize me. What he knew or suspected, I can only guess at. I was baptized and I was adopted at the same time. I officially became Mirosława Maria Łączkowska. This child, this identity, resides deeply within me.

CATHOLICISM

At the age of nine, I went to communion and confession. Although it was a tedious ordeal, I loved every moment of it. Mostly I loved the idea of getting dressed up like a princess. My mother wrote to a friend outside Antwerp, Belgium who sent us beautiful material for a communion dress, which a dressmaker made for me, and a gorgeous crown. I felt like a princess with matching white suede shoes. So much better than sneakers with chalk coating! It was wonderful. As young as I was, I didn't like going to confession. The Łączkowskis were not strict Catholics, but they were traditional. They kept the holidays even though they didn't go to church regularly. It was relatively easy for me. Even during the Communist regime, when the church was separated from the government, one still had to go to church on holidays because of the neighbors. The social environment required it. We were very much Communists. I belonged to the Communist youth party, the ZMS, short for *Związek Młodzieży Socjalistycznej*, the Socialist Youth Union. It was the youth faction of *Polska Zjednoczona Partia Robotnicza* (PZPR), the Polish United Workers' Party (Marxist-Leninist). Of course I hadn't any idea what I was doing, but I had to belong there. There was no choice.

Everyone had to belong.

I went to church because everyone else did, but the older I got, the less I liked church. The emphasis on miracles somehow disturbed me. The priests cried out from the pulpit, "Sins and sins... and sins!" I could not relate to these scoldings. We were children. We had yet to accumulate our sins. We did nothing even vaguely sinful, really. We were good children; we were good girls.

We always made sure to go to the handsomest priest for confession. There were stories about him having affairs with women. He always seemed to have very young housekeepers.

There was one priest we especially loved who left the church because he'd had an affair with a woman and fathered a child with her. He later moved to Chicago, then Detroit. Many years later, I looked him up, just out of curiosity, but I didn't contact him.

Some of the priests from my childhood in Poland were very old-fashioned. When you went to an older priest for confession and said, "I was not nice to my mother," or "I talked about somebody," sometimes the priest would become angry and rush out of the confession booth. Even as a child I felt such displays of anger were unprofessional.

Though I was a naïve child, I felt that absolution granted by a priest made no sense. I still feel that way. I thought of the building caretaker and other miserable neighbors who had denounced us, then receiving absolution, and felt the injustice of it. I said to myself, "How can you go to a priest and get absolution for your sins from him? Who is he to give you God's forgiveness?" I believed this could not be. He would tell you, "Okay, pray this prayer three times and then this prayer four times, and then you're forgiven." Thus, in the end there is no real consequence. This makes it easy to commit the same sin over and over. For sure the ritual did not speak to my heart.

As a child, I often felt comforted by Catholic religious practices, statues, and prayers. I always felt Jesus was my friend and I needed a powerful friend, as much as or more than most children, I suppose. But as the years went by, I became ever more skeptical of many Catholic practices. First of all, I said to myself, "I think

I'm intelligent. But I know nothing about sex or marriage or being a parent. So how can a celibate priest talk to us of these experiences? Where is he coming from? How could he possibly know? How could he ever be an authority?"

When I became old enough to start dating, even though there was never any sex involved, I found going to confession brought out even more negative feelings toward these religious rituals. At confession, our priest asked me questions that seemed wildly inappropriate. If I told him, "I kissed a boy," he wanted to know "What kind of kiss? On the cheek? On the lips? Open mouth?" I was embarrassed and confused. We didn't do anything even remotely like what the priest was describing. People of our generation didn't have sex of any kind. But then the priest would ask, "What else?" It felt as if he was perversely enjoying questioning me about details. It felt demeaning to me.

I began to recoil from the Catholic religion. To me there was little personal meaning in our priest's sermons, especially regarding everyday life. I felt a dishonesty undermined his words. He preached of sin but he seemed to me no model of virtue or piety.

Of course there are fine priests today and if you find a young, highly educated priest, then you'll surely hear some genuine and wisdom-filled sermons. Every year I entertain about sixty people in my house—hidden children like me, hidden from the Nazi Holocaust by righteous Christians, and their spouses, for a Chanukkah party. At one of these get-togethers we had a Jesuit priest from Poland. He was a bright man who had a Ph.D. and was lecturing at the University of Michigan. This is the type of priest who has much of genuine human value to impart. I felt that he talked about life just like the best of our rabbis.

SCHOOL

By the time I started elementary school, my mother had found work, and things were better for us. Money was tight, but I began to get a government scholarship, what they call a *stypendium*. I was

I Was a Hidden Child

Elementary School, Sosnowiec, 1955

a half-orphan because I no longer had my father, Józef. Orphans could receive the *stypendium*, but they had to have good marks in school. The amounts were not as much as students get in America, but they were a little bit, and every small addition to our finances helped us greatly.

My schools were co-ed. We wore uniforms: navy blue smocks made of a thin material. The smocks had white collars which got dirty easily and had to be taken off and washed every day. We let them dry overnight. After ironing the collar in the morning, we sewed it back on. It took two seconds because we used big stitches. I don't know why we were we so foolish and worked so hard. Didn't we have snaps? It seems no one ever thought of that.

I finished elementary school and went to a high school called Bolesław Prus, which was named for a famous Polish writer. We still had to wear uniforms, and the teachers were like gods. When any adult came through the door, especially professors, everyone immediately stood up straight. You couldn't answer him, couldn't tell

Elementary school, Sosnowiec, 1955. Mira is holding the ball.

him how you felt. It was an autocracy with no dissent imagined or expressed.

We had one teacher, Franciszek, who was particularly severe, but fair to his students. His last name was Hanzel. He was young, maybe in his thirties, and he was strict. I liked him because he taught me so much about Polish grammar. All the students went on large group overnight field trips, which he chaperoned. He was a lot of fun though his requests had to be obeyed.

In chemistry, I loved the teacher, so I did well. The math teacher was a drunk. He never explained things correctly, so I never learned the basics and always had a problem with math.

I was not the stereotypical nice girl who sits quietly and obeys all the rules. I was not the type of girl who would listen to the teachers without question. I got into trouble but luckily, I was a good student. They tolerated me because I contributed in other ways. By the time I was 17 or 18, I was engaged in a lot of school activities. And always busy with dancing and singing.

We belonged to clubs at school. I belonged to an amateur

Mira (first left) in folk costume, Podgrodzie, 1955

drama club, *Co Proszę*, "What's Your Wish?" and we performed mostly in student coffee houses. There was so much singing and laughing. We sang popular Polish songs and we sang American songs like *Diana* by Paul Anka and *Only You* by The Platters. Some American songs were translated into Polish.

The person in charge of the drama club, Dzidek Rezner, was one of my best friends. He died of Lou Gehrig's disease in March 2005, at the age of 67. Fred and I saw him just the December before. Dzidek's death was a shock, his loving presence suddenly gone—a thread of my life fabric now missing forever.

Dzidek was married to one of my good friends from elementary school, Grażyna. I am still close to her. As adults, Dzidek and Grażyna took care of my mother when she was in need. They helped my mother move into a new apartment and made sure she was comfortable.

The teachers appreciated my involvement. I remember when they needed someone to write about Lumumba, a controversial anti-colonialist leader in the Belgian Congo. The teacher talked about him like a god because he was viewed as a Communist. I volunteered to give a presentation about him. One former teacher, Mrs. Tokarczyk, told me, "After you left the high school, it was like after Jesus. There was nobody like you ever again."

Miriam and her boyfriend Waldek, Pogoria, 1959

That beautiful compliment stunned me, the comparison so extreme, and made me feel happier about my past. Possibly this was what Mrs. Tokarczyk intended. There are angels, often well disguised, who see us with loving eyes.

In childhood, we experience the world as magical, vibrant,

alive. Sadly, we lose our natural sense of wonder as we grow up. When I was busy with life events I gave little thought to my birth parents. But this has changed. Though I have no conscious memory of my birth mother Faygel or my birth father Shlomo, they enter my dreams where they are real to me as if I know I'll see them again. And what could I possibly say to them? There are no words that are adequate. And so I accept their love and try to love as powerfully as they loved me.

Our school curfew was strict. Being spotted with a male friend outside school was risky. You'd have a lot of explaining to do. If a teacher saw you walking on the street with a male friend after ten o'clock on a Saturday night, even if he was not your boyfriend,

Miriam and her friends, Sosnowiec, 1959

even if he was your own brother, the teacher would humiliate you the next day in front of all the students. Even worse, if it was a school night, forget it. You'd never recover from the torment you'd get. Because the weekend curfew was ten o'clock, we never stayed out late. I'm telling you, life was wonderful but somewhat restricted. Compared to what American kids have today, we had no freedom.

For my generation, sex was a taboo subject. We didn't mention it. We didn't engage in it. We held hands, put an arm around each other, and maybe, rarely, kissed. That was it. We were

Miriam and her friends, Sosnowiec, 1959

all unquestioningly committed to being virgins until the day we were married. At curfew, I might be right in front of our apartment sitting on a bench, by the beautiful park, looking at the mysterious and sad weeping willows, playing the guitar with friends, and my mother would look through the window. She would call out to me, "Mira! Are youuu theeere?" and I would answer, "Yeees, I aaam." She didn't worry, as long as she knew I was there.

Sosnowiec was an industrial city, so we would go by train out of the center of town to have a picnic by the water. We brought a guitar, a couple of bottles of cheap wine, and we had a great time. I smoked Sport cigarettes. They had no filter. But it didn't really matter because I never learned to inhale. Very rarely did I smoke in

At a pinic in Pogoria, 1959

front of my mother in the apartment. She allowed me to, and she smoked with me.

My friends also smoked cigarettes. We drank wine. A few times we stayed out past curfew and escaped detection. We never drank to the point of being drunk, but the wine and cigarettes of course made us feel grown up. An adult might have said these transgressions made me a rebel, but they happened naturally. When somebody brought a bottle or two of wine, we all had a glass or two. If someone had a pack of cigarettes, we just smoked them. We were naïve by today's standard, but we weren't perfect. We all had our moments.

Waldemar

DATING

I was dating guys before I was 16, but not the way people date now. In those days, we dated in groups. We'd go to the movies or meet in friends' homes and throw parties for ourselves. It is true, there were always "bad" girls. But as for my friends, we socialized in groups.

When I was 16-years-old, I knew a boy, Waldemar Bala, and we were in love; you might say, "puppy love." Notwithstanding our mutual affection I still would meet other guys. So in effect, Waldemar was just the most special of all the guys in the universe of my affection. It was not like in America where you "go steady" with that special someone. We didn't behave like that. Our relationships were not as serious as that. We called it dating, but as often as not either person was at the same time dating someone else. Sex was not involved, not even contemplated, so it was altogether a different kind

I Was a Hidden Child

of dating. I never had serious boyfriends even as I got older because by then I had come to realize that I could not stay in Poland. I had to leave Poland.

Waldemar, here at age 40, was my first teenage crush
Sosnowiec, 1980

I have stayed in touch with Waldemar and his family and visited with him every time we traveled to Poland. My children met him on our trip there in 1985. I introduced him as my "first boyfriend."

Waldemar helped my mother with whatever she needed after I left Poland. He died in 1989 when he got hit by a bus while crossing the street. That was a traumatic shock to me. Waldemar was in the inner core of my most cherished childhood friends and one with whom I had been in contact over the years. I'm still in touch with his sister Hania. We talk on the phone all the time. I'm also in touch with Waldemar's daughter Dorota and her husband Janusz. They visited us in the United States some years ago.

Mira, Sosnowiec 1959

It was not always to a picnic spot out of town that we escaped for our picnics and get-togethers. Strangely, we would often walk to cemeteries for our gatherings. We would talk there and sometimes maybe even kiss, untouched by any reluctance due to the nature of our surroundings. No one but us was ever in the cemeteries at night. In the dark there was a peaceful calm, a serenity that we felt. Cemeteries in Poland were always, and are still, filled *in the name of God* with flowers. They also contain beautiful mausoleums. It's an almost artistic experience to visit a Polish cemetery.

SHADOW OF A DOUBT

When I was eight or nine, I became the target of anti-semitic remarks. Not from adults, but from children, children from my neighborhood, in the back courtyard of our building. They kept calling me "Jew" and "dirty Jew." Everything was Jew, Jew, Jew, Żydówa, Żydówa.

Naturally, I approached my mother with questions, and she kept saying, "Don't worry about it. You are beautiful. You look like a Gypsy. You have blue eyes and dark hair. They don't know what they're talking about. Just ignore them." I came to her in tears many times: "Why are they calling me a Jew?" One time she got so mad, she told me, "If someone says you're a Jew, you tell them, kiss my ass." That's how mad she got.

When you're eight, nine, even ten or 11, you take your mother's word. But then, at some point, you start thinking. By the time I was in my teens, I knew there was something different about me. And the teasing continued.

Every time I went out with a friend on a date, some kids in the group kept on calling me "Jew." I still had no knowledge of my true past, no inkling of my birth parents who had perished in the Holocaust. I just had an eerie sense of a kind of hidden identity within myself though I couldn't describe or understand it. I just didn't know for sure if I was Jewish or Catholic.

The mothers of my boyfriends seemed to love me so much. But when they too began to suspect that I might be Żydówa, Żydówa, they no longer thought me so wonderful. I had no idea of what a Jew was, nor any impression of Jewish people growing up. If there were Jews that we saw, they never had long earlocks of hair. They never wore skull caps. Jewish people in Poland looked no different than any other people. They were modern. It's true that they lived in certain neighborhoods before the war, but I never knew a Jew. Of course there were almost no Jews to know after the Holocaust. Those who hadn't perished in the concentration camps usu-

Mira at age 16, 1958. Beginning to discover my birth identity.

ally hid their identities and did not appear ethnic in any way. So I didn't know who they were and had no picture in my mind of Jews.

The first time I learned anything about Jews was as a child at Easter. We were warned not to go onto the street because, we were told, "Jewish people are gonna kidnap you. They're gonna kill you, and they're gonna drink your blood. They need your blood for matzah." (Blood libels are allegations that a particular group kills people as a form of human sacrifice and uses their blood in various rituals. The alleged victims are often children. Blood libels against the Jews were a common form of anti-Semitism during the Middle Ages, though there is no ritual involving human blood in Jewish law or custom). The older people, including most of our neighbors, said this. But I never heard it in my house. Of course, my mother never said such things.

Though my mother kept encouraging me to ignore the teasing, a shadow of doubt hung over my identity. It depressed me, troubled me, and stirred confusion in my heart.

MOMENT OF TRUTH

The first significant event affecting my personal identity occurred when I was 16 years old, just before Easter of 1958. The Poles were repeating the infamous blood libel that Jews were killing young children for matzah. Poland remained, after the war, an anti-Semitic country. My mother felt both sad and vulnerable in the face of this hatred of Jews. The holidays arrived, the heartache came, and that year she was especially low on money. She couldn't give me what she wanted to provide for me, neither food nor clothes. Whatever stipend, or *stipendium* I received, was quite minimal.

I remember standing in the doorway to the kitchen one day, when, out of the blue, my mother stared at me and cried out, "You and I are such orphans." I looked at her, confused, but wanting to comfort her I answered, "*Mamusia*, I don't feel at all like an orphan. You give me everything you can and everything I need." The only birth certificate I had ever seen said Mirosława Łączkowska. Adoption was a taboo subject, and she never talked about it. This was the first time she had said I was an orphan.

What made her talk about it? Starting in 1956, there was a huge emigration of surviving Jews leaving Poland for Israel. She was afraid that if she did not tell me, someone else just might. Someone from one of those agencies she feared might very well find me again, sit me down, and tell me the whole story, the truth about my past.

So Stanisława, the only mother I ever knew, the bedrock of my life, my security and my identity, sat me down and told me. She recounted my personal history, bit by bit, sort of backing and filling much of what I've written here. She told me exactly what had happened, how she took me from the ghetto, how she imagined she would have me only for a few months, how her family had sacrificed to keep me safe, how deeply she loved me as much as her own children, and, most difficult of all for her to relate, how my mother never came back for me.

She told me about my uncles, she told me that maybe the men who had visited were only pretending to be my uncles. She said they were in America, and she didn't know much more. As far as I know, my uncles and my aunt never contacted us. It is true that they later came to think of me as family, but for all those years they never tried to help me or to help my mother. If only they had sent even three dollars a month between the three of them, it would have been a wonderful help. But I suppose that they never thought of it, never thought about us or helping us after the one frightening and unsuccessful attempt to bring me to America.

THE GYPSY

The month before my 16th birthday, a sort of wandering Gypsy fortune teller came to our home. I heard a knock and opened the door to find this strange and mysterious-looking gypsy woman who asked to come in. Of course we had almost nothing to give away and I certainly didn't want to give anything to Gypsies. My experience was that if you gave them a sandwich, they would throw it out. Gypsies were a part of life in Poland, living on the edges of society. Often they would settle in an open field just outside of town. They sent their kids out to beg. If you gave them bread instead of money, they would smush it onto the walls. They were not hungry. They simply wanted money, and if they didn't get it by asking, they would find another way.

This Gypsy girl came to read my fortune and she wanted money. I was scared. I didn't welcome her in. I told her to leave. I started to close the door in her face. She became angry and blurted out, "You're gonna die on your 16th birthday." Then she turned and left, realizing she would get nothing from me.

Sure enough, being vulnerable and naïve, on my 16th birthday in May, the birth date my mother had chosen for me by counting back from the day she took me in from my birth mother, I became frantic. I refused to leave the house and didn't go anywhere that day. My friends all had to come to my house. It was only when midnight struck that I calmed down and breathed a big sigh of relief. Surviving my 16th birthday was the first reason 1958 was a significant year for me. There was another event that felt profoundly personal and important to me.

MRS. CESARZ

In the summer of 1958, a few months after my 16th birthday, something happened that left an imprint on my memory. I would go with my mother and nieces to a village every summer. It was a true village, primitive compared to our town. There were no electric lights. I felt it was like life had been a hundred years before.

In this village, there lived a tall slim woman in the house next to ours. She must have been about 40 years old. Her name was Mrs. Cesarz. Her husband had left her and she lived alone. I remember she looked quite skinny and walked very straight. She had a cow and she walked it into the open fields to graze. Every year we went to this village where the skinny lady and her cow lived. When I was 13, and later 14, my friends were continually making fun of her because she seemed so thin and so frail, and her cow used to jerk her along. I never made fun of her. To me she was a curiosity and I didn't know what to make of her; she was different and interesting, for sure. But even though I never joined the others in making fun of her, even though I was a leader and was in a position to stop it, I did nothing

Mrs. Cesarz's house, Kuźnica Mała, 1958

to stop the others, all of my friends, and sometimes I too laughed at her antics. I cannot explain my inability to step forward and tell my friends how wrong it was to make fun of another person, especially a woman alone in the world. Maybe I just couldn't overcome the pressure to go along, or not to criticize. Whenever the cow jerked her she screamed at it, *Ty kurwo, ty kurwo!* "You whore, you whore!" Sometimes I laughed too. We were foolish and mischievous kids sometimes. As I grew older, though, I actually befriended the skinny widow and heard some snippets of her life and her past, mostly sad memories.

But during the summer of 1958 we arrived in the village and did not see Mrs. Cesarz out and about as usual. I asked about her but nobody had seen her recently. I was my usual inquisitive self, and since I had gotten to know her a bit, I went to knock on her door. The door was ajar. I walked in. She must have been what I considered a wealthy woman. I saw that she had some very nice down comforters and that certainly confirmed it in my mind. But Mrs. Cesarz lay in bed, looking seriously ill. She was dirty. She was wearing dirty clothes, and sleeping on dirty linens. Her hair was a mess.

So the first thing I did was to chop some wood and light a fire in her stove. I waited for the stove to get hot. It didn't take long because I had put a lot of dry wood in the stove bottom. Then I brought some ice-cold water from the well and heated it on the stove until I could fill a large, old laundry barrel. I eased her slowly out of bed, brought her over to the hot water, and washed her hair. I knew that whenever I washed my own hair, I felt like a new person. It was all I could think of to do for her. Of course we had no such thing as shampoo then. I just used soap that I found in her house. And as I

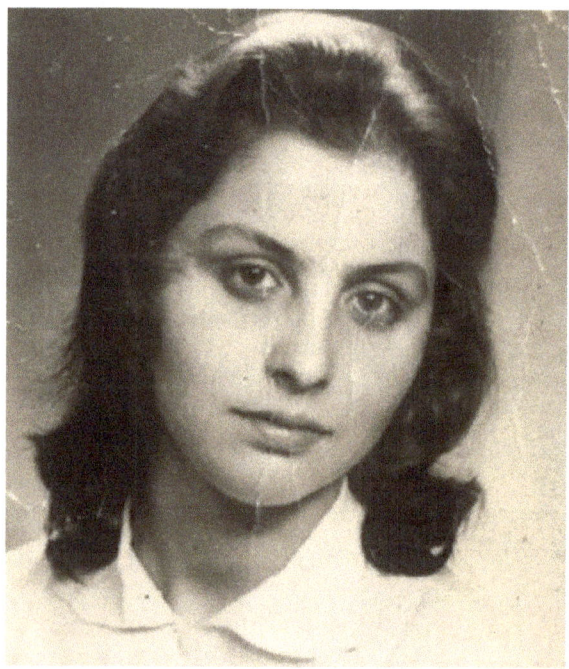

Mira, Sosnowiec, 1960

combed her hair, I was astounded at all the lice just falling into the water. So I carefully combed through all of her very thin, fine hair and then I washed her again until finally she was lice-free to my eyes. Then I made two little braids of her now clean hair.

I took her slowly back to her bed and fluffed up and arranged her pillows. I didn't change the linens because I didn't know how to do it in this village.

Suddenly she sat up in bed and said to me, "I bless you. I bless you my dear child. I thank you for doing this for me. May you live to 100 years! May you be happy and healthy! May you have a wonderful husband and children!" Whatever sacred and loving words are in the Polish language, she used them all to bless me. My mother had made some soup or something for Mrs. Cesarz two days later, but before I could bring it over, a neighbor came to tell us that she had died. I had no words. I cried. Stanisława had tears in her eyes, knowing how I had tried to save her, and she hugged me.

People in Poland don't seem to come to weddings or to parties, but when there are funerals, just about everybody comes from all directions, from near and far, and they put a lot of emphasis on the wake. Mrs. Cesarz was laid out in her own back yard for the wake. I'll always remember that day in every detail. Flies were everywhere. The body smelled. They buried her after three days. I always think of her as my guardian angel because she blessed me so powerfully, so sincerely, so extravagantly.

MIXED FEELINGS

The slow and steady unraveling of my identity as a Polish Catholic girl, the incremental, step-by-step discovery of my birth identity, the slow emergence of the awareness that I was not born a Catholic with Catholic mother and father, but that instead I had Jewish birth parents, caused me, as it dawned on me, no small amount of confusion. The slow process of unraveling my self—my Catholic self which was me from infancy and was all that I knew—and allowing into my mind a new and different self—a Jewish self—and weaving this into my conscious awareness, created in me no end of confused and mixed feelings.

I've heard the odd expression, "I'm of two minds about that," and suddenly, increasingly, that expression described me. On the one hand, with part of my mind, so to speak, I was relieved because I had known something was not right, unnatural. And now, suddenly, all of my discomfiture, my unease with Catholicism started to make more sense. I so detested the confessions that for this alone I was relieved to believe now that I was Jewish. But I feared change. I feared the unknown and anything Jewish was unknown to me, or known only from the perspective of a Polish Catholic. Except for church rituals, I was comfortable where I was. I loved my mother deeply, more so for having been ripped away from her and forced to devise my own means to return to her; I loved my brother, my sister, and my nephew. We had warm and loving family times together. So in that way I didn't want any changes and I feared there would be some difficult and confusing adjustments now that I was merging into this new identity of experiencing myself as a Jewish self instead of a Catholic self.

Despite my resistance to change and my fear of the loss of my immediate family, I had become increasingly aware that there was no future for me in Poland as a Jew. Of this reality I was ever more acutely aware because of all the anti-Semitic remarks I encountered. As the recognition of my past and my birth parents became clearer to me, I increasingly wove this new reality into my social encounters. Now when I went on a date with a guy I told him right away that I was Jewish, even though I knew as little as he knew about what that truly meant. But whatever being a Jew implied, for better or worse in their eyes, I knew deep within that this was the true identity I had never consciously known. I had grown used to the scene when I was walking on the street with my date somewhere, that a child or somebody would be calling me all kinds of names. People would just scream out things like, "Oh, look, the Jew is walking!" It was a small city. Today the population of Sosnowiec is about two hundred thousand people, but in the 1950s, it was maybe eighty thousand,

Identity Transitions

Bolesław Prus high school, Sosnowiec, 1959

greatly reduced from the immediate pre-war years. The population was 127,000 before the German occupation. Back then, everybody knew everybody.

At school, I used to recite poems. There was one poem that I performed, *Koncert Jankiela*, for which I won a lot of awards. I went to Katowice and Warsaw to perform it in competitions. *Koncert Jankiela* is part of *Pan Tadeusz*, the 1834 epic poem by Adam Mickiewicz whom many describe as the Shakespeare of Polish literature. It's in the twelfth book of the series (in Miriam's *Collected Works* of Mickiewicz it starts on page 236). Mickiewicz also wrote *Dziady*, a play about a beggar (in 1968, Polish authorities banned the

Ludwik Wilczynski accompanying Mirosława in Pogoria, 1959

theater production of *Dziady* at Warsaw University, claiming the play was anti-Soviet). The action triggered student protests that were met with severe reprisals. The Communists, under Premier Gomułka, blamed the Jews for producing *Dziady* and for being anti-Communist. *Koncert Jankiela* is about a Jewish man who played the *cymbały*. (The cimbalom, or santouri, is a musical instrument found mainly in the music of Hungary, Romania, Moldova, Greece, and Ukraine. It is related to the hammered dulcimer of Western Europe.) I did not choose *Koncert Jankiela* because I was Jewish, at least not intentionally; I just chose it because I liked it. Soon after I found out I was Jewish, I happened to recite this poem in a class, as I had many times before. There's a line where Jankiel says to General Jan Henryk Dąbrowski, "General, you are so precious—we have been waiting for you, like we Jews wait for our messiah." I said this line with such feeling, and I remember the history professor commenting, "You know, you perform it so very well. This is because you're Jewish." It might have been intended as a compliment, but I felt it as if it were an anti-Semitic insult. She emphasized the fact that I was Jewish, and I felt deeply wounded. How strange that I had absorbed the pain of being a Jew in a culture that often demeaned Jews, though I still had little idea what a Jew was or what it meant to be a Jew.

Mirosława with high school friends in Pogoria, 1959. Pogoria is a place to relax and swim, a sort of weekend resort in Zagłębie Dąbrowskie, southern Poland, near Katowice and Sosnowiec.

Despite my worries about the future, I also knew there were going to be positive changes. I didn't develop an inferiority complex as I discovered and adjusted to the reality that I was Jewish; rather, I imagined I was suddenly somehow blessed in various ways. The knowledge that I no longer had to believe in Catholic miracles or in the sacred stories of the immaculate conception relieved my mind as I had struggled to accept these tenets of Catholicism. In that way, many of my doubts about Christianity were now made unimportant to me personally as my self-discovery unfolded and the Jewish identity became my new reality. So even though I didn't want any changes in my life, I was in many ways relieved. Eventually I took to Judaism, not because I had to but because Judaism felt more real to me at a personal level.

My slow discovery of the truth about my identity, my Jewish family, and my past put into a different perspective the many questions I'd had about miracles, about Catholic rituals that I couldn't understand, and about my personal unease regarding Catholic ceremonies and practices. I was happy to be discovering a new reality in place of my doubts and unease. What a relief that the customary knot in my stomach, I guess from swallowing doubt and confusion, now vanished. Nonetheless, still being in a totally Catholic world and feeling I had no choice, I continued to practice Catholicism outwardly both at home and away from home, but just until I was out of school. I reassured myself that it was only a matter of time.

My mother Stanisława also knew my world had changed and that there would be no future for me in Poland as a Jew.

CHAPTER FOUR
LEAVING POLAND

In 1960, my father's two brothers and his sister suddenly decided to take action. They had lived in America since 1947 and even though I had not heard from them all those years, they hadn't forgotten me. In 1959, Rabbi Menachem Mendel Schneerson, the world renowned *Lubavitcher Rebbe* living in Brooklyn, New York, spoke fervently about the urgent mission of sending holy emissaries, *tzadikim*, to Poland to find hidden Jewish children and to offer them assistance to live Jewish lives—assistance to come to America where they could be nurtured and taken care of. Hearing this message,

Left to right: Mala Hirsch, Mirosława Łączkowska, Rabbi Irving Hirsch. Tatra mountains, Zakopane, 1960

my uncles Yisrael and Jacob, and also my Aunt Hanka, awoke to this urgent task of finding Jewish children who'd survived the war and were living in the homes of righteous gentiles in Poland. They immediately decided to take action.

THE HIRSCHES

It was my 18th birthday, May 26, 1960, and my mother heard a knock at the door. There stood a handsome man, as she would later describe him, clean-shaven, in a black suit and black hat. His name was Irving Hirsch. He came with an interpreter, an older man named Mark who spoke Polish. I don't know whether it's a coincidence or divine destiny that it occurred on my birthday, or at least the date my mother Stanisława had chosen as my birthdate. When Mr. Hirsch arrived, I was downstairs in front of my house with Waldek, one of my boyfriends. We had been at some kind of a meeting, he had walked me home, and we were chatting. My niece Hania came downstairs and said that there was somebody waiting for me and that I should return home right away. I walked back into the building and up to our apartment, and as I walked in, I saw these two men.

Mr. Irving Hirsch introduced himself and said that he had come on behalf of my uncles and brought their regards. My mother was shocked to see a young, handsome man come for a visit on behalf of my uncles. She was already thinking, "Uh-oh, he's probably taking her to a whorehouse or who-knows-where." She was deeply disturbed, frightened, and clearly upset about it. Mr. Hirsch tried to explain that he was a respectable family man, with a wife and children, and that his intentions were honorable and pure. When my mother was in the kitchen, he spoke to me directly and he encouraged me to leave Poland for the United States where I could better my life.

It was fraught with danger to even think about talking to someone about religion, or America, or Israel, and most certainly about leaving the country. Poland was a Communist satellite of the

USSR. Irving Hirsch and the interpreter understood this well, yet were willing to jeopardize their own lives to save me, as they saw it. They could have been imprisoned for this mission and the keys tossed away. Yet they displayed no fear, acted as perfect gentlemen, shook hands with my mother and kissed her hand, entirely in keeping with Polish custom.

Mr. Hirsch had completed his mission, having offered me the alternative to leave for America, so he returned home to Belgium. Then about a month later, he returned to us, this time with his wife Mala. It struck me as humorous and cute that she called her husband Suki. On his first visit to us, Hirsch had seen my mother become frantic, terrified really, and so he knew it would be absolutely necessary that next time he bring along his wife to reassure Stanisława that no evil plans were afoot. Mala had been born in

From left to right: Hershele Hirsch, Mala Hirsch, Simele Hirsch. Brooklyn, New York, 1960

Łódź and she spoke beautiful Polish. It turned things around for my mother to see this handsome 20-something-year-old man with his lovely and intelligent wife, and realize he was a family man. My mother became very comfortable with Mala. Despite all that, she still would not allow me to leave Poland by myself.

During the first or second visit to our apartment, Mr. Hirsch told me secretly—again when my mother was in the kitchen—that he'd like to meet with me alone. There were no telephones, so he just told me a time and a place we would meet.

He always met me in a park, never in a crowded place. He would describe his plans, always speaking to me through his interpreter. He wanted to bring my mother and me to Belgium. I thought that the Hirsches lived there and were just inviting us for a visit. I later found out that they had moved there from New York just in order to rescue me and other hidden Jewish children.

Mr. Hirsch left me some Polish money to make telephone calls to him from the post office. I corresponded with him through the address of another Jew in Sosnowiec. They were all working together. It was nearly impossible to get visas to America, but the plan was for us to join them in Belgium for a visit and then plan from there. My mother struggled with the idea of going to Belgium. There were moments when she would say, "Fine, let's go," and there were other moments when she would change her mind and resisted the whole idea because she was frightened. I would say, "Mom, we have an opportunity to travel. Just to get out of the country would be wonderful." Few people living in Poland flew on airplanes back then, but the Hirsches had plane tickets for my mother and for me. To us, going to Belgium seemed as real as going to the moon, but at last my mother agreed.

A NEW SONG

There was no airport in Sosnowiec. We took a train to Warsaw. On the train, I met another girl who was traveling. She was with a group going on vacation. They sang an endearing folk song over and over.

It took about three hours to get to Warsaw, and the girl let me use her guitar so I could learn and play along.

Trzy Kwiatki (Three Flowers)

Na drogę życia dostałem dwa kwiatki:
Od przyjaciela i rodzonej matki.
Więc myślę sobie: mam dwa kwiatki świeże,
Teraz się dowiem, kto mnie kocha szczerze.

Najpierw uwiędły kwiatki przyjaciela,
Potem uwiędły dwie gałązki ziela.
Kwiatki mej matki pozostały świeże,
Bo tylko matka kochała mnie szczerze.

For life's journey three flowers I have gotten.
From my true friend, from father and mother.
I thought, now that I have three fresh flowers
I will see who loves me truly.

My true friend's flower withered first.
After father's flower, the two little twigs withered next.
But Mother's flower stayed fresh,
for a mother's love is true forever.

I was so moved by this song, and it burned into my heart. My mother's flower stayed fresh, indeed. Were it not for her strength, heroism and love I would not be here today. It is my anthem of love and represents a simple truth that has framed my journey and echoes in my heart. This is the song that I sing to my grandchildren.

BELGIUM

When the Hirsches came to Poland they showered attention on me, took me to concerts in Kraków and the Tatra Mountains in

Zakopane and so on, and they thoughtfully befriended my mother. My mother placed all of her confidence in Mala because she saw us developing a true friendship. There was not that much difference in age between Mala and me. She was a Polish Jew. She was about 27; I was 18. She had two children. In 1961, Mr. Hirsch and Mala really pressed me to leave Poland. They kept writing letters: "Come, come, come!"

I was determined to leave anyway, and they kept urging me. Finally, my mother gave in and we applied for visas. The travel rules were not so strict between Belgium and Poland and on July 15 we left for Belgium. As far as we knew, we were going for a vacation and we felt fortunate. We wanted to arrive on a Saturday, but they had to explain to us that it was a holy day, *Shabbat* (the Sabbath).

We flew on Sabena Belgian airlines. My eyes widened to see the airline stewardesses were so slim and beautiful. At that time, stewardesses had to be tall and thin to be hired. We were served what seemed to me an elaborate meal on the plane. We were poor, so for us it was exquisite. I don't remember exactly what was served, but I do remember vividly what they served us for dessert. We got fresh oranges and I was stunned and thrilled. I could hardly believe that there was one orange for my mother and one orange for me. I felt awestruck. I had never had an entire orange to myself. On rare occasions my mother would buy an orange, just one orange for the entire family. She'd carefully peel it, make sections, and serve everyone their own small portion. Oranges were so expensive and rare that when we bought an orange the saleslady would ask, with concern, "Oh my, who's sick in your family?"

But now on Sabena Airlines we had whole oranges to ourselves and we stared at them, hesitating because we didn't know how to start eating them. Then, all of a sudden, the stewardess surprised us and, before we could interrupt her, she took away our trays with the oranges, apparently thinking we were done.

We couldn't communicate with her. I'd studied Latin and Russian, but not French or Flemish. I just burst into tears. But the moment was gone, as were our oranges. Funny how this moment

Leaving Poland

still resonates in my memory over all the decades and life events since then.

At the airport in Belgium, an unexpected reality struck us. The handsome and secular looking Mr. Hirsch whom we knew from his visits to Poland now appeared as an Orthodox Jew. We were taken aback and, unaccustomed to interacting with Orthodox Jews, were uncertain about how to relate to him. There he was greeting us at the airport in Brussels with *peyes* (sidelocks), and dressed formally and somberly, like a pious Jew. He had a black hat and a beard, and he no longer offered to shake hands with us. Before he had been the charming and secular looking Mr. Hirsch. Now he was Rabbi Irving Hirsch. He had two polite and beautiful children with him at the airport: Hershele and Simele. His wife Mala, it turned out, was a very religious woman, with a *sheitel*, of course—a wig covering her own hair for modesty. It was a beautiful *sheitel* and no one would have known it wasn't her own hair.

We traveled from Brussels to Antwerp and went to the Hirsch's beautiful apartment at Belgelai 93 on the eighth floor. On the balcony was a basket filled with oranges and grapefruits. A wonder! I used to get up in the middle of the night to eat them. I rewarded myself with these fruits and really enjoyed them while watching all the American cars go by. It was fascinating to see all the Chevrolets and Cadillacs with their huge fins, or wings.

Antwerp was a beautiful city, with a population of 12,000 religious Jews. Some were *Satmar* (a very religious Orthodox sect), some just Orthodox, like the Hirsches. I lived at the Hirsches' with my mom for six weeks.

During the first few weeks in Antwerp, we were entertained constantly and met many kind and interesting people. I was introduced to the Chief Rabbi of Antwerp, Rabbi Chaim Kreizwirth. Did he ever look to me like Moses! Rabbi Chaim Kreizwirth and his *Rebbetzen* (rabbi's wife) Sarah befriended me. He was a very Orthodox man but he looked at me unflinchingly, straight into my eyes. It surprised me that he did not cast down his eyes as had other Orthodox Jewish men I'd met.

Rabbi Chaim Kreizwirth

Rabbi Chaim Kreizwirth was born in Kraków and spoke beautiful Polish, as well as English, and Yiddish. We were often at the home of Rabbi Kreizwirth where, on *motzei Shabbat* (after the Sabbath), Saturday evenings, he and his wife hosted exciting and interesting conversations about Judaism and a lot of reminiscing about life. He was not only the chief rabbi in Antwerp, but also a world-renowned scholar. People came from many other countries to hear his talks which he delivered in Yiddish. Whenever he spoke, if I could understand the language, I sensed his deep perception of life and his gentle wisdom. He was a true *tzaddik,* a righteous person. He initiated many programs to assist vulnerable people, the poor, widows and orphans, the sick and infirm.

Through July and August of that summer, the Hirsches kept us occupied with wonderful activities. There was a magical park in Antwerp with wonderful walks among stately old trees and beds of flowers, a park that seemed to me a world apart and reminded me, in its spiritual presence, of the willow park opposite our own apartment. We visited the park often and also traveled and discovered other places. They took us to Brussels, Amsterdam, Rotterdam, and to an island off Amsterdam that seemed enchanted to me.

Rabbi Kreizwirth and his wife patiently guided me in Jewish customs and practices, all the time mindful of my mother and respectful toward her. We enjoyed Friday evening Sabbath dinners weekly in the Kreizwirth home. I loved when the rabbi made *kiddush* (the blessing over the wine). They drank wine with my mother and weren't concerned that she might pour me some. To me at the time, and looking back, it felt the Kreizwirths erred more on the side of making us feel welcome and loved rather than on the side of strict adherence to Jewish laws, though I'm sure these were observed. Without fail, and from the goodness of their hearts, they treated my mother with genuine respect, recognizing her bravery and self-sacrifice in caring for me through the war years and postwar years. They recognized her righteous nature.

Experiencing life as a Catholic for almost 19 years helped me, perhaps surprisingly, to appreciate Jewish religious strictures, Jewish rituals, and Torah laws. The more I learned and the more I discovered about my Jewish heritage, the more I loved the Jewish world view, the theology, the customs, and the lifestyle. For many years I had struggled with what seemed to me to be the continual reference to miracles as occurring in our everyday lives. So I felt especially relieved to learn that in Jewish thought, everyday events and historic events were not always explained away as miracles. I was fascinated by this new world of Torah and wanted only to learn more. I spent hours learning with Rabbi and Rebbetzen Kreizwirth. They hold a special place in my heart.

MY MOTHER'S FEAR

Suddenly, one day out of the blue, the Hirsches proposed that I go to America as an exchange student at Stern College, the women's college of Yeshiva University in New York City. I could leave shortly, just as soon as I could obtain a visa.

At that turning point, my mother became frightened, imagined losing me forever, and she started to have a change of heart. She could not bear to part with me and wanted me to return to Poland with her. She didn't want me to stay in Belgium. She feared I'd leave her and forget about her. Little did she know, I could no more forget her than my own name. She was my mother, the only mother I ever knew, or remembered. I always remember with love everybody who was in my life in Poland. Yes, I remember them all. Making the experience more excruciating for us were the problems with my visa. Delay after delay frustrated the plan. My mother often broke down from the conflicting emotions of wanting the best for her daughter, fearing her loss to a faraway country, and having my hopes rise and fall. She cried often and so did I.

One *Shabbat*, we were walking up the stairs. Because it was *Shabbat*, Jews did not use the elevator, but of course my mother could. She was waiting for the elevator downstairs in the lobby. She saw that the Hirsches had a letter in their mailbox. If it was about her daughter's welfare, she was willing to bend the rules. Someone had opened the letter for Rabbi Hirsch before *Shabbat* was over so he could read it. Well, it was written in Polish and it got into my mother's hands.

The letter came from the translator Mark whom we had met when Rabbi Hirsch came to our home in Poland that first time. He was writing to detail and explain how much money he had spent on each child "rescue" case in Poland. He detailed what he'd done for each child and how much Hirsch owed him. There was a list of children he'd discovered and worked to bring to Jewish homes. And there I was on the list. Me, Sława, Lucia, Cilia, Anna… He had compiled a detailed and legitimate accounting of money, time, and expenses for every child. If you were unaware of the intent, an intent arising in the name of God, to bring the children to safe Jewish homes, you might suspect the expenses represented the cost of child kidnappings, for whatever purposes you might imagine. And my mother imagined the worst. She became convinced by this evidence of multiple child "rescues," and the costs of each, that there were evil purposes involved and at the very least that this accounting of costs of moving children from their homes proved that these people were using us. She didn't believe for an instant that the movement of children was undertaken in the name of God. Quite the opposite! She felt the people involved, nice as they appeared on the surface, were part of an illegal business activity, stealing children for who knows what ultimate purpose, and she threatened to go to the police. She threatened to report that they were stealing young people from Poland.

My mother didn't understand the idea of taking Jewish children from their Polish parents and bringing them to religious Jewish homes and therefore back to the Jewish faith, in the name of God. She had believed I'd be coming back to Sosnowiec with her, even though she also realized that I had no secure future in Poland. In a sense, she wanted to have her cake and eat it, too. If she really hadn't wanted me to go, she could have said no. In 1961, few people left Poland. It had seemed an exciting prospect, but things were not going her way. Having almost lost me more than once, my mother was always nervous about us parting and she endeavored to be with me or near me all the time. When I took private English lessons at the Berlitz school, she would sit anxiously in the waiting room counting the minutes. She feared I might never come out, that maybe school was really a pretense for something else and I was not really studying. She became agitated as her fear got the better of her. In her mind, the Hirsches and their "accomplices" were in the business of selling me, and other children, not "saving" me or the others. Her worst fears were not baseless, just misdirected. It was a reality indeed that many girls were abducted by criminals, taken to whorehouses, and their lives destroyed, just as today human trafficking continues and often goes unpunished or undetected.

When my mother threatened to go to the police, the Hirsches became frightened. After all, what they were doing was not really legal, even though they did it to rescue, as they saw it, Jewish children, all in the name of God, following a Jewish commandment to rescue Jews from non-Jewish influences. Despite my mother's misgivings and protestations, their efforts to "rescue" me intensified.

BECOMING STATELESS

We were surprised when suddenly the Hirsches asked us to go to a salon for an entire day at a spa. What we did not imagine was that they told the spa to keep us there all day for pedicures, manicures, perms, color, and massages.

While we were there, Rabbi Hirsch took my passport from under the mattress and provided it to Belgian authorities to apply for a *titre de voyage*—a travel document allowing me to enter and exit Belgium as a "stateless person." (This type of re-entry permit was provided under the 1951 Geneva Convention for Stateless Persons.)

Polish people quite commonly hid valuables under their mattresses and the first thing one did when returning home was to check under the mattress and make sure everything was there. When we returned from our spa day, my mother checked under the mattress and could hardly believe that my passport was missing. But it was. She screamed. Then she screamed again. Instead of explaining to us the difficulty of getting a visa without my Polish passport, the Hirsches had just taken it. They were afraid my mother would have objected, so they helped themselves to it. The heist seemed to me balanced by the reward of a document that provided me with a new freedom of movement. Even though I was still required to get a visa from every country I wished to visit, at least now I could apply for a visa to the United States.

SEPARATED BY HIRSCH

Following the passport heist, my mother and I fell into a pattern of continually crying and arguing about my uncertain future, and our uncertain future. She simply could not imagine life without me. I felt the same about my mother but for me there was also the sad reality that I couldn't imagine any kind of happy life in Poland. We argued, cried, reconciled, made decisions, and rescinded decisions. We experienced such maddening changes of heart, especially my mother's heart, that it drove us both to depression. We soon felt we were just existing, not truly living life, and certainly not enjoying life. The Hirsches could not help but notice. They suggested an outing to visit my mother's friend, far from Antwerp on the French border. Rabbi Hirsch and his American friend Mr. Gross traveled with us and left us with my mother's friend for a few days, hoping the changed environment would help us recover our spirits.

After three or four days, Mr. Gross and Rabbi Hirsch came to bring us back to Antwerp where Mala and their children were waiting for us. Back in the Hirsches' apartment, when the visa topic came up, my mother didn't want to hear about it. Rabbi Hirsch gave her $1,000 for expenses so that she could stay with her friend as long as she wanted before returning to Poland.

One day, my mother and I were in our room playing a card game called *Thousand*. My mother had just won and was laughing with me when Rabbi Hirsch came in and gave us the news, "Mira finally got her visa to the United States." My mother fell silent and so did I as our happy laughter gave way to solitary thoughts about an unknown future.

ORPHANED AGAIN

Two days later we were packed and went to Brussels Airport. It was the end of August. The Hirsches and their children were my traveling companions.

At the airport, my mother and I were both hysterical. We just couldn't stop crying. I'll always remember my mother's face, her pain and fear and, most of all, profound sadness. I parted from her so abruptly. I can still hear Hirsch rushing us, "We're so late! We're so late! Say goodbye!" I believe he felt it would be better not to prolong the parting. He didn't want a long goodbye. But the rush to separate from my mother left a terrible pain in my heart. We held each other closely. And oh, how I kissed her face and her hands, as we were forced to release each other, not knowing if we'd ever see each other again.

We finally parted. All I felt was loss and the tears on my cheeks. I knew my mother was feeling the same, even worse. I sat with the Hirsches in the terminal for forty-five minutes waiting for the plane. We boarded, but in just over an hour, we landed. We landed in Zurich. I was shocked, even frightened. I had thought we were flying to America. Why were we landing in Zurich? I became nearly frantic and hollered, "Mala, where are we really going? I'm an adult, you know."

She looked at me and said in a soothing voice, "I'll tell you the truth. We're in Zurich and we're going to go to Montreux. We'll stay there until your mother leaves for Poland, and then we'll return to Antwerp. You didn't get the visa yet as an exchange student, but we felt we had to separate you from your mother. The situation became impossible. We just didn't know what else to do. You were crying, she was crying." Mala tried to reassure me, telling me that after I left my mother could return to the airport.

They didn't trust me completely, and they were afraid that maybe I would go back with my mother, so they once again used deception to control me. And, once again, I felt tricked. All the manipulation and deception, all the anguish was once again resurrected, as they were rescuing me in the name of God. We took a train to Montreux and took up residence in a beautiful apartment overlooking Lake Geneva. I experienced terrible heartache and sank into a deeper depression. Whenever I left the house and saw a mother with her family, I would think of my mother, my family in Sosnowiec. It made my agony worse; I cried my heart out every day and felt frightened and alone. I cried because they didn't trust me and because they had tricked me. I cried because I'd left my mother, because the goodbye was so sudden. I could hardly hug her. The sudden loss of my mother was foremost in my mind. I felt helpless and all alone. I cried because I didn't know how I would ever again visit Poland, or ever again see my mother. I cried because they had stolen my passport and now I was stateless. I didn't have Polish, or Swiss, or Belgian citizenship. I cried because I didn't know what the future would bring. All in all, I felt now that I was truly an orphan, once again an orphan. And this time there was no adoptive mother to rescue me. I was truly all alone. Even though I was an adult by any reckoning, I felt more like a twice-orphaned child.

It was 1962 and I was 18 years old. I felt alone and couldn't believe I'd been separated from my mother. I missed Antwerp as well. I had already made friends there and met people I liked. I had even made some male friends. One was an Israeli, one was Polish. Neither boy was religious and so they didn't count as marriage prospects, nor was there any romantic aspect to our friendships.

Offsetting my sadness in Montreux, I experienced the Jewish holidays for the first time: Rosh Hashanah, Yom Kippur, and Sukkot. Rosh Hashanah fell on Friday, September 28, 1962, and Yom Kippur fell on Sunday, October 7, 1962. The Jewish year was 5723. We were invited out for holiday meals by Orthodox families living in Montreux. We were welcomed everywhere. The Jewish community invited us in with open hearts.

Eventually I came to realize that Mala Hirsch was a pious woman. She was like an older sister to me. She was delicate, thoughtful, and kind. She taught me so much about Jewish customs and traditions. Her children became the focus of my life. But for their friendship and love, I don't know how I would have survived. I played the guitar and sang for them. Mala taught me my first Jewish song, a Shlomo Carlebach song. I was so very proud to learn the song, play it on the guitar, and sing it. Singing Jewish songs, I felt an inner healing. One of the songs included the famous verse from

I Was a Hidden Child

Psalm 121, Essa Einei El Heharim Me'Ayin Yavo Ezri. "I shall lift my eyes to the hills whence will come my salvation."

After my mother visited her friend outside Antwerp, the Hirsches were advised that my mother had returned to Poland. We must have been in Montreux for six weeks by then. I returned to Belgium, traveling by myself by train from Montreux to Zurich and then by plane to Brussels. The Hirsches did not return to Belgium with me. They went to their home in America, mission accomplished.

At the Brussels airport, I saw the American Sherman Gross, a wonderful man, as I later discovered, waiting for me. He was with a younger man, Aaron Lubinsky who spoke Polish. I already knew Aaron. He had translated for my mother and me when Mala Hirsch wasn't around. He took me to the movies once, too. He was Belgian and a modern Orthodox Jew who understood our mentality. Rabbi Kreizwirth wanted him to marry me very much, but I didn't like

Sherman Gross, Sarah Gross, Miriam Ferber, Fred Ferber
Far Rockaway, New York, 2006

Aaron in any romantic way. His brother was a *hasid* (Hebrew: Hasidic—a pious Jew living according to the mystical teachings of the Baal Shem Tov) and wouldn't even look at me.

THE GROSSES

I felt fortunate and relieved to live in the home of Sherman Gross and his wife Sarah. Sherman and Sarah were a young American modern Orthodox couple with real common sense and grace. Sherman was in Antwerp for business. He was in the feather business. Sherman and Sarah had three children—two girls—Gitty and Sandy—and one son, Melvin. They took me in as one of their own.

Sherman and Sarah's home was open to all the girls and boys who were refugees from Poland, who had grown up in Catholic homes rescued by righteous Christians, and we all felt comfortable in the Gross's home. Their refrigerator was always open to us and there was always food on the table. Even though they were just starting their lives together, they were generous. Of all the people we met, they were different because they felt to us more like our contemporaries. In the beginning, it was hard for us to talk to them because we didn't speak English, but Sherman and Sarah were kind and patient. I absolutely adored their children.

Most of the Polish Jews in Belgium wanted to help us, but they also wanted us to become *hassidim*, whereas Sherman and Sarah knew we couldn't go from one extreme to another. Sherman and Sarah understood our Catholic upbringing more than anybody. Rabbi Kreizwirth also understood our upbringing, but he couldn't express his understanding of those differences. He was Chief Rabbi of Antwerp and only spoke to us about certain things.

But Sherman was very honest and open with us, the "hidden children" who had grown up as Christians in the homes of righteous Polish Catholics. He knew that we were never going to become Hasidic. He knew that we were not accepted among *Hasidim* because we were not dressed properly. It seemed our dresses were always either too short, or too tight, or too revealing of our figures. Sherman understood and he and Sarah accepted the reality of our past.

During that period, I was deeply troubled that I had to lie to my mother who believed that I had gone to America. The ruse meant that I had to send my letters first to a person in America who then sent them to my mother in Poland. Of course, my mother, believing I was in America, also sent her letters to America and they were sent on to me in Belgium. The deception was anguishing to me and wasted many weeks between letters.

At least there was never a question about the cost of international postage. Sherman always had stamps in his drawer. "Miriam," he would say, "just use as many stamps as you want. Write as many letters as you want. Please! You don't have to ever ask me." Sometimes I was embarrassed because I used so many stamps sending letters to America, which were rerouted to my mother in Poland, I missed her so.

Despite the sense of homesickness for my mother and my prior life, I felt fortunate to live in the Grosses' home. Having spent time in a strict religious environment, I was relieved that the Grosses were less strict, more modern. They were observant Jews but not as if they came from another century.

I remember being in Antwerp for the Torah holiday of *Simhat Torah* (*Simhat Torah* fell on Sunday, October 21, 1962) which celebrates the love of the Jewish people for the Torah. We went to a very religious synagogue. The fervor of the holiday was obvious and intense. Carried away by the outpouring of religious emotion, I went to dance with the Torah and, not knowing that men and women do not dance together, I just went straight into the middle of all the men, somehow missing the obvious, that I was the only woman there. I soon learned! They hollered, "*Schnell! Schnell!*" (Quick! Quick!) and pointed me to the door. What did I know? But I caught on quickly and rushed off toward where the women were gathered.

Soon after crashing the men's group, which seems amusing now but was embarrassing at the time, I began an intense study program in all-girls classes led by Rabbi Kreizwirth. In these classes I met many girls and young women who had also been "rescued" from Poland. Some returned to their Catholic families in Poland because they were unable to relate to the rabbi or to the Jewish lifestyle. Others, who were intrigued by the idea of a Jewish homeland, made *"Aliyah"* (going up) to the young state of Israel. Eventually I was the only one waiting to leave, waiting for a visa to America.

Sherman and Sarah Gross opened their hearts and their home to all the Polish girls in a way that brought us close without overwhelming us. They knew and understood that having grown up

Miriam's daughter Shari Ferber Kaufman, Papa Chiel Freilich, Erna Freilich. Benai Barak, Israel, 1986

Erna Freilich, Benai Barak, Israel, 1986

as Catholics we could not possibly make a transition from a Christian upbringing to suddenly become Orthodox Jews or *Hasidim*. They were so thoughtful and communicated no expectations of us to conform or to accept any religious restrictions we weren't ready for.

PAPA AND ERNA FREILICH

During my time in Belgium, after my mother returned to Sosnowiec, I met a religious Jewish couple, Erna and Chiel Freilich, and they felt to me like guardian angels. I called them Erna and Papa. Just being in their presence calmed me and made me feel a little less lonesome for my mother Stanisława and "home." I spent most Sabbaths with them.

Papa and Erna had already had a Polish Jewish girl stay with them, Anna, but she had returned to Poland, unable to bear the social pressures, the religious rituals, the many changes from life in Poland. The Freiliches didn't want Anna to influence me, so they waited to invite me until after Anna had left.

I lived with the Grosses but spent many Shabbat dinners (and *motze Shabbat*) at Erna and Papa Freilich's home. They had four children: Miriam, Charlotte, Leo, and Avrom. I often played guitar with them. Papa was a deeply religious man. He wasn't as modern as Sherman Gross, and yet he was a lot of fun. Papa was scholarly and pious. He would not go to the movies, yet I would sing for him, although Papa generally did not listen to women sing. But I was the exception because he treated me like a daughter, and so he allowed me to sing all my Polish songs in his presence. The Freiliches were also from Poland and they understood my personal history and background better than most.

Miriam Ferber and Papa Freilich, New York City, 1964

Papa was in the diamond business. He was a *Hasid*, to be exact, a *Gerer Hasid* (Hasidic Jew originating from the city of Ger), and every Shabbat he wore a fur-trimmed hat, a *streimel* (Yiddish: A round fur hat worn by certain *Hasidim*). Before the war, his father, a rabbi from an elite family of scholars, was widely known and respected in the Jewish community in Ger. Papa was meticulous in his grooming, but unlike most Orthodox rabbis, he did not have a beard at that time. Papa was unique in his outlook and sometimes would speak about the Kabbalah and Jewish mysticism. He was such a bright man that when he spoke people felt deeply moved, enchanted really, and they craved more interaction with him. He was a charismatic man.

We had much in common, including Polish as a common language. We talked at length about life experiences. We talked about Erna's childhood in Katowice, a town close to Sosnowiec. Papa was born in Kraków. They both had seen it all—the horrors of World War II. Both Papa and Erna were concentration camp survivors.

I loved being with Erna. She was smart, beautiful, elegant and had endured terrifying life experiences. Every month she would spend her German reparation money on girls like me, hidden children from the homes of righteous Polish Christians who had never experienced any Jewish education or influence. Even though she had four of her own children, she bought us clothes and anything that we needed. She used her own money to buy me so many things, like shoes, dresses, coats. Even after I left for America, I stayed in touch with her. I thought of her as my guardian angel, just as she was an angel to all the girls who were in need.

They kept me busy while waiting for my visa and we traveled. They also sent me to travel with a girl from America who was five years older than me. We drove in a Volkswagen to places like Paris, Luxembourg, Lugano.

Eventually, the Freiliches moved to B'nai Barak in Israel. We still keep in contact with their children today. Once, Papa came to our home in Michigan. I'd invited a lot of friends and we were all talking. It was already about one o'clock in the morning, and everybody was preparing to leave. But when Papa arrived, my friends stood in the hallway talking to him and they just couldn't leave. They spoke to Papa for another three hours. It was almost four in the morning when they left. He radiated a kind of openness, warmth, and personal magnetism, and his words felt deeply personal and real. His appearance was immaculate. He was altogether a kind, beautiful, and imposing presence.

Papa and Erna are now deceased. Three out of four of the children remain, and sometimes I speak to them. As a kind of guardian angel, Erna also really took care of me. She and Papa, along with my husband Fred, made my wedding. Erna had the most beautiful wedding gown handmade for me, replete with pearls. And Erna got us a beautiful sterling stemware set as a gift. She was a powerful presence in my life until the day she died. I miss her and I miss Papa. When I'm in Israel I visit their gravesites—the Freiliches and the Kreizwirths.

SŁAWA

When I lived in Belgium, I met Sława, a beautiful girl from Bochnia, Poland, a small town on the river Raba in the south of the country, between Tarnów and Kraków. She was another of Rabbi Hirsch's many hidden children. Before I left for America, Rabbi Kreizwirth said to me, "You know, I'm going to send you to Israel. Go to a kibbutz (a communal farm) for a month, and you'll have a wonderful time." I didn't go, but my friend Sława did. Before she left, we took a picture together.

Sława was an intelligent girl who played guitar and piano. She had guys around her all the time whereas I was more reserved and distant. I was a "good girl." But there was one time we got crazy. We were walking in Antwerp, looking for something to do, and we decided to go to a church for confession, a natural part of our lives in Poland. But this time we'd go as a joke. Antwerp is Flemish and French but we were Polish. I asked, "What's the difference? The priest doesn't speak Polish." We laughed, thinking ourselves awfully clever.

Well, let me tell you something, the priest didn't speak Polish. But he said, "Just wait a minute," and he went into his office and brought out a book, written in Polish, that listed all the sins. All you had to do was point at your sin, and it was translated into his French and Flemish. I started to laugh hysterically, nervously. Sława and I changed our minds and when the priest turned his back, we ran out of the church! He outsmarted us. I couldn't believe that he was fully prepared to take confession using a Polish-French-Flemish manual. Sława, another Jewish child brought up as a Christian to save her from the Nazi Holocaust, actually hated the Jewish religion. She was almost a Jewish anti-Semite. I don't blame her for the animosity she felt for being torn away from her family, just as I had been. What happened to us was neither fair nor just, even though, from the point of view of those who "rescued" us, it was unavoidable. Our "saviors" tore us away from our lifelong routines, growing up in a Polish Christian environment, and they dropped us into the homes of Orthodox Jews, *hasidim*. We were suddenly and constantly surrounded by a very heavy version of Orthodoxy that was completely unknown to us and entirely ignored our upbringing. They wanted us to be religious, but they didn't know how to teach us slowly; they expected radical change, immediately. The *hasidim* were also in a way co-opted in this process of finding homes for hidden children and often hesitated to open their homes to us fearing that the way we dressed and behaved could affect the value systems established in their families.

I adapted to the changes very well, not because I had to, but because I wanted to. I was so dismayed by the rituals and thought patterns of the Catholic religion at that point that I yearned for a change and intensely wanted to be Jewish. I loved the Jewish religion. I took to and loved the customs and the warmth of being among all those religious people. They started to dress me like them and I did begin to wear long sleeves and long, modest dresses. Perhaps also the myriad of rituals and customs of Polish Catholic life prepared me to enter into a world of customs, habits, rituals, even though radically different in style and motivation. The women wore beautiful and realistic wigs, for modesty, called *sheitels*, and many of the Rebbetzens I met wore diamonds because their husbands were in the diamond business.

Sława did not adapt so well. Rebellious and unaccepting of

strict Orthodox customs, she used to go up to little children with long earlocks—*peyos*—and pull them, just as any Jew hater might, though she knew well that she herself was Jewish and born of Jewish parents, who had perished in the concentration camps. Her rebellious behavior was terrible, a sort of extreme reaction to the rapid and unexpected changes in her life as part of being "rescued." They feared sending her to America in part because they thought she would marry out of the faith. So they suddenly shipped her off to Israel. Their aim was to gather Jewish orphans, marry them to other Jews, guide them to become religious, and of course hope they'd have many children—many Jewish children to replace all those lost in the Holocaust. I think Sława married a Sephardic Jew. She sent me a picture. She was performing as a singer with her husband in Israel. We eventually lost contact.

In Israel, Sława met a reporter who wrote her life story, along with my life story and included a picture of us in an Israeli newspaper. Our amusing moment of fame was to have repercussions.

"BE MY DAUGHTER"

A week after the story appeared in the Israeli newspaper, Rabbi Kreizwirth called me up. "Miriam, you've got to come to my office," he said. "A man who claims to be your father is here."

People suffer in many ways. We all know hope. And we all know despair. There is no life unmarked by both. No one person's despair or joy is greater than another's. And yet, there is, and it seems always will be, war, and with it, extremes of both. Though I was born amidst immense suffering, I escaped much. I escaped terror and death thanks to the bravery of my mother and father—the bravery of both of my mothers, and both of my fathers. By war's end I had lost a mother, a brother, a father, and a second father. Stanisława was my rock and my security who treasured me so that she even allowed her own daughter Wanda to suffer in a kind of strange exile to protect me, to hide my Jewish birth and heritage. Sometimes I have felt over the years an inner anguish that I rarely express to anyone—an anguish that I let her down somehow when I left her to make my own life where I felt a safer future awaited. Yes. People suffer in many ways. We flee despair and run toward hope and every generation I believe has its regrets, whether avoidable or unavoidable.

I went to Rabbi Kreizwirth's library and saw a gentleman with gray hair, and a sense of sadness about him, his eyes looking as if he were lost, or unsure somehow, looking almost defeated by life, I felt. He looked at me across the room, as if from across an ocean, then opened his arms to me and cried, in a plaintive voice, "Hello, hello, hello, my daughter Miriam."

I looked at this man and saw how desperate he was. He had traveled all the way from Israel just to see me.

"Are you sure you're my father?" I asked, gently. "What is your name?"

"Mączyk," he replied. He got that right.

"But many people have that name," I challenged him. "Well, I had a daughter...," he told me.

"And in what year was she born?" I asked. "1939," he sort of mumbled.

"I'm so sorry. Mr. Mączyk. I'm so sorry." I started crying. I felt my breath catch in my throat. And in a hushed voice I said, "I was born in 1942."

But Mr. Mączyk could not let go. With tears in his eyes, matching my own, quietly he pleaded, "Let's say you're not my daughter, okay, so," he took a deep breath, "then, please, you can be my daughter. You can be my daughter." His loss was so vast, his hope so fragile, the truth so cruel, so disheartening, he could not let go. I didn't know what to say. Then it came to me. "You can't do that," I replied quietly. "You should call my uncles. Perhaps you are one of the brothers."

He appeared broken in spirit; he looked so small at that moment. All at once I felt sorry for this man, sorry for the loss of my parents, even sorry for myself. But from the moment I'd walked into the rabbi's study, I knew he wasn't my father. For me there was never a doubt. Just sorrow, for us both. When Mr. Mączyk left the rabbi's office his grief would trail him, I felt sure, as he walked away from his one last hope, on a rainy afternoon in a strange European city, profoundly alone, the rain and mist shrouding his heart.

Nonetheless, telephone calls were made, back and forth. Mr. Mączyk accepted that he was indeed not a member of our family. He took one last chance after speaking to my uncles and said, "I told everybody in Israel that I'd found my daughter. And I so, so wanted you to be my daughter."

You know, if I had been a four- or five-year-old, it might have been different. But I was not. I was by then 19 years old. I hugged and kissed him, sympathized with him, but I said, "You know, I really do have blood relatives in America." This sad memory remains vivid to me because it is so universal. Hope is often tinged by loss. He had lost his daughter. I had lost my parents. We met with a vain hope, dashed first for me, then for him. We were united in grief, though not in family. Many stories just like this unfolded, during and after the war.

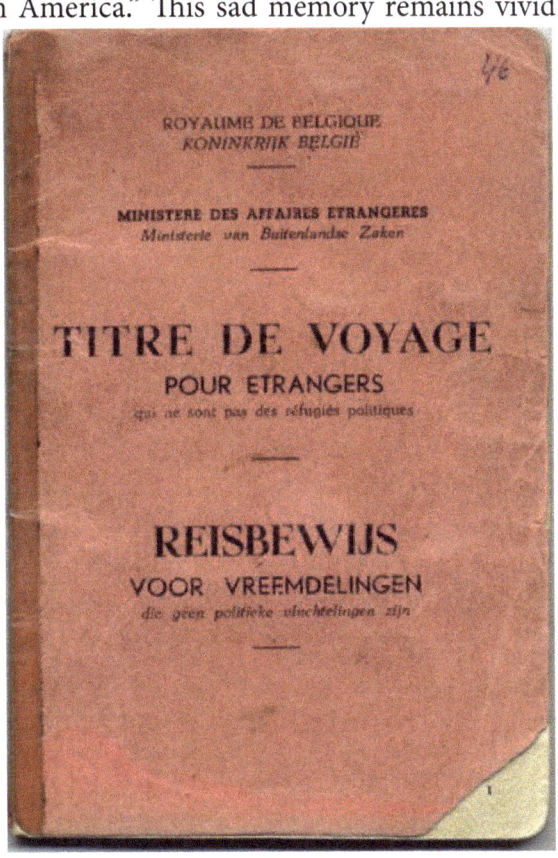

Travel document

GOODBYE PARTY

I guess that in the march of history there's always a first and a last. For me, I was the last. I was the last "hidden child,"

Travel document

the last child "rescued," in many cases from brave and loving Christian families who had risked life and liberty to save Jewish children. As far as I know, I was the last to leave Belgium. One of my friends left for England, one left for Israel, one left for Holland. But my destination was America and I awaited the hardest visa of all to get—to the United States. When it finally came through, my friends hosted a farewell party. All the religious women and their husbands, the people I had befriended, gathered at the Gross's home, many bringing presents, and we reminisced about my stay in Antwerp. I played guitar, and we sang. We exchanged addresses, promising to keep in touch, which we did for a long, long time.

I was 19, leaving for America and a bit scared about leaving. Hardly anyone ever left to go to America and I had never even heard of anyone from Poland going there. Yet here was that visa staring at me from my passport and it just hit me that I was really going.

After a lot of goodbyes and tears, I left Antwerp with

beautiful memories of a time of growth and maturing. I felt I was now standing strong on my own, ready for a new life in America and ready to meet my Jewish family and see the pictures of my mother and father that I had been promised.

I had so many packages, maybe seven or eight different hand packages, and it hadn't occurred to me to put my belongings in one suitcase. A mother's expertise would have been handy, but of course I had to learn on my own. I somehow managed with all the packages on the flight to America. I was on a journey to the United States—more than just a physical journey, it was an emotional journey and I was unsure of my future. Where and with whom am I going to live? What will my uncles and the rest of my family be like?

I was religious because I had been taught by those who had

Arrival in the United States, at the airport, New York, 1962

intervened to bring me out of Poland and into a Jewish environment. As years and decades have gone by, my view of Judaism has changed and I feel more spiritual now, more reflective, than in those early years. I now feel connected to God and to Judaism more from an inner longing rather than outward teachings. Connection to God is more than just religious observance. I believe that rituals without a genuine and personal connection to God falls short of what it means to be religious. We all change inwardly over our lifetimes. Looking back, we may easily feel that what we took to be observance, may well have been more about confused ideas of youth and conformity than about deep inner conviction.

CHAPTER FIVE
AMERICA

I know now that the watershed event of my life, obtaining a visa for me to come to the United States, required a certain diplomacy. The stamp in my passport shows Ruth Schneider was Consul General of the United States in Brussels. Mr. Gross, leaving no stone unturned, went to the American Embassy, invited her to dinner, and somehow used his influence to get me the visa. It was granted on February 15, 1962 and on February 18th, I left for the United States.

At US Customs, I was seriously interrogated as a citizen of a Communist country. I had taken only a few English lessons at the Berlitz Language School in Belgium and it took me a while to explain. I started to tell them why I had been in the Communist Party,

*Arrival in the United States, at the airport, New York, 1962
Mira is with flowers*

explaining that it was mandatory. We had no choice. There was no option to refuse. At last, they let me go.

There were so many people waiting for me at the airport. I saw my uncles. Though they were strangers to me, I kissed and hugged them. I recognized the Hirsches. I loved them and remembered all the kindnesses they had extended to me and my mother. Rabbi Hirsch, Mala, and the children had returned to America six months before, and they were all waiting for me at the airport. At least thirty people had come to the airport to meet me and soon filled my arms with flowers. My uncles had told the neighbors and I was overwhelmed by their greetings. One of the couples there was Lorraine and Cantor Shalom Nelson who befriended me from day one.

LORRAINE AND CANTOR SHALOM NELSON

I noticed a beautiful couple, handsome and tall, and she wore a gorgeous black hat. She was introduced to me as Lorraine. Her husband Shalom was a cantor. Lorraine and Shalom Nelson befriended me. This lady was very special; she radiated love and warmth.

I spoke little English, Berlitz School basics. I appreciated how clearly Lorraine spoke, slowly pronouncing every word. They took me under their wing right away. They were religious, observant in every way, but modern Orthodox. He had no beard but he wore a hat. She always wore a hat, not a *sheitel*. They became my guardian angels in America. The Nelsons took me into Manhattan for the first time to see a show at Radio City Music Hall. My English was good enough for them and I understood them as well.

Lorraine empathized with me about being separated from my mother. She was compassionate about the reality that I felt so close to my Polish family. She never called them *goyim* (gentiles). On the contrary, she understood and recognized their bravery. In her eyes, my mother was a hero, and she told me that all the time. Unlike some other people, who dismissed my Polish family, she was very compassionate, and she really and truly made my mother

Shalom and Lorraine Nelson, 1962

appear to be a courageous hero to me. I played guitar for them and sang Polish songs even though they didn't understand them.

Shalom died in 2008. Lorraine is very much alive and holds a special place in my heart.

NEW YORK

In America, I lived with my Uncle Jacob (the younger of my two uncles), his wife Mania, and their three sons Abe, Benny, and Shayke. Their apartment was in Canarsie, Brooklyn, off Rockaway Parkway.

It was not easy. I went to school and worked. When I first arrived, I spent two or three weeks at Beis Yaakov, a women's seminary in Crown Heights. It was a strict Orthodox community, not modern. Hebrew and Yiddish were common. I soon realized that the local girls' seminary wasn't for me.

I had received my visa on the premise that I would attend

I Was a Hidden Child

My aunt and uncle, Mania and Jack Mączyk, Carnasie, Brooklyn, New York, 1967

Stern College in Manhattan which I thought would be a better place to learn English. I commuted there. It was ten minutes by bus to the subway and then forty minutes to Lexington Avenue.

HARLEM

One day I exited at the wrong station and found myself in Harlem. I had no idea where I was or what to do. I approached a young and strong-looking black man and told him, in broken English, that I had gotten lost. He smiled, told me not to worry, and gently took my hand and led me back to the right subway. In Europe I never saw black people and after this encounter I was excited about learning to

At Uncle Jack's and Aunt Mania's house where I lived in 1962. Canarsie, Brooklyn.

live in New York with its diverse people and cultures.

SPECIAL RECORDING

One day, Shalom Nelson came to me and said, "Miriam, I have a surprise for you. I'm going to do something for your mother. I'm going to make a phonograph record of you singing to her." We made a record of all the Polish songs my mother loved and sent it to her. The record contained many beautiful songs, especially *Trzy Kwiatki* (*Three Flowers*), the song I first heard on the train to the airport in Warsaw. The song and record were a hit in Sosnowiec. My mother told me that all my friends would visit her to listen to the record. That was the best gift she had ever received. Sadly, after my mother passed away, I never found the record.

LEAH AND MOISHE KATZ

I was very rarely at my uncle's house over Shabbat. Since many in the community thought of me as a "diamond from Poland," they set about introducing me to eligible guys. Every Shabbat I went to a different home. Many thoughtful people befriended me. Most often I

Moishe and Leah Katz, Detroit, 1986

spent Shabbat with Moishe and Leah Katz and their three daughters. They were, like the Grosses in Belgium, modern Orthodox. Their home was open and welcoming to everyone in the Jewish community.

Shabbat dinner at their home was a spiritual experience. We had long discussions, even with my broken English. Leah cried her heart out as she heard, in my broken English, the story of how my birth mother gave me to Stanisława, how my parents and brother then perished in the Holocaust, how Józef died because of the house search which turned up the shortwave radio, how I grew up never knowing who my birth parents were until my teen years, and how my adoptive parents and siblings had sacrificed for me, to protect me. She was deeply affected by the story, mine and others like mine, even as the wartime losses and heroisms receded in many people's awareness. The Katzes were like a slightly older sister and brother. When Rabbi Kreizwirth came into town from Belgium, or when Papa Freilich came in, Leah opened her home for them as well. I added them to the list of my guardian angels.

My *shidduch* (match) with Fred played itself out in Leah and Moishe's home and culminated with our *Tannaim* (pre-nuptial vows) in their basement. Rabbi Kreizwirth had flown in and it was beautiful.

JEWISH CHOICES

Though I was an observant Jewish woman, I was confused about the nature of Jewish life. In America, I was introduced to Jews who lived Conservative and Reform lifestyles as well as some who were entirely secular. Being Catholic for so many years, I deeply appreciated the reality of being Jewish. To me the Jewish religion felt real, made sense, but I never knew that I had choices other than strict observance. In Belgium, I saw only Orthodox observance, but in New York, I saw less strict alternatives. Questions arose in my mind. It was difficult being Orthodox and I felt increasingly uncomfortable in this lifestyle. I loved Judaism and traditions, but I did not want to be strictly Orthodox.

In front of my aunt Hanka's home. Left to right: Miriam Ferber, Mania, Hanka, Jack Mączyk, Shari Ferber Kaufman, Detroit, Michigan, 1968

Today, we observe Shabbat but also feel it's okay to drive to the synagogue, and I would never bring anything unkosher into my home. I love making big Shabbat dinners at home, and I enjoy Orthodox synagogues, but also feel comfortable in a Conservative synagogue. I love being Jewish and feel grateful to have been returned to my roots.

UNCLES AND AUNT

In New York, I lived with my Uncle Jacob, or Jack, the younger of my two uncles, and his wife Mania who was deeply religious. Though my uncle wanted to give me the impression that he, too, was religious, I found out later that his observance was more about teaching me than following it himself, and learned that he had a tough time with his wife's religious intensity.

My other uncle, Yisrael, nicknamed Srulek, held a special place in my heart because he had been so close to my birth father. Srulek told me stories about my family, in effect giving me back my past, or at least glimpses of my family's past. He wasn't religious and didn't pretend to be. He remarried after his first wife died of cancer. He had problems raising his two young children and his second wife was mentally unstable. He had his own troubles and, in a sense, had

My aunts and uncles wit my family. Standing: Fred Ferber, Ronny Ferber. Sitting: Annette Ferber, Shari Ferber, 1967

a hard life. But I felt at ease and comfortable in their home.

My Uncle Jacob later told me that he was the one who had come with his friend after the war to visit my Polish mother. Yisrael, the older brother, had received the note from my Jewish mother, hidden in a shirt collar, that instructed Jack where to find me. My Polish mother Stanisława did the right thing keeping me with her. My Uncle Jacob and his friend Motek were young people and had just come out of a concentration camp. What would they have done with a four-year-old child?

Shortly after I came to America, my Aunt Hanka from Detroit visited me in New York. Together we left for a short visit to Detroit. As we got to know each other, I asked her if she had tried to find me. Though she said she had inquired about me in Poland, I didn't believe her. I'm not resentful, but I do wish they had reached out to us with some form of help. They had been in America since 1947 and though not wealthy, they had become established. A tiny amount, three or four dollars each month, would have spared us much heartache. Used clothes from neighbors would have made a world of difference.

I hear others' stories now at the Hidden Children Organization conferences—stories of how aunts and uncles and friends of deceased parents traveled to fetch hidden children or to help somehow. At last my uncles and aunt did wake up and act, but only after an American lawyer, who must have been inspired by the vision of the *Lubavitcher Rebbe*, Menachem Schneerson, became determined to save all the Jewish souls he possibly could from Poland. If Dr. Yaacov Griffel hadn't done this, I would probably still be in Poland. In hidden child support groups, when I spoke of my uncles and aunt, many in the group exclaimed, "Tell them how you feel. Tell them!" But I explained to them, "There's no use now in telling them." And I never told them how I felt. Never. Because I loved them and respected them. My daughter once went to see Uncle Srulik and he cried, "I'm so sorry for what we've done. We should have done more for your mother." I don't blame him. He had his own problems. His wife, though only about thirty years old, died of cancer in 1956, leaving him alone to raise two children.

When we see poverty in America, we may not be able to imagine what poverty was like in post-war Europe or in many areas of the world today, with no safety net for people, and starvation not uncommon. We always could afford to eat but we scrimped and fought daily to do so. My mother often used dry leftover bread to make a soup. What kind of soup? She boiled water, put in a little lard if we had some and a little garlic. Then she cut the dried bread in cubes and added it. That was our soup. She could afford to buy a quarter pound of meat for a weekend. I wished that my aunt and uncles understood this.

I tried to tell them how poor we were, but it was by then unnecessary and I felt I could not explain to them the reality of our life in Sosnowiec. My aunt told me that they wrote to my mother and she wrote back to say that she didn't want any contact. But I knew this wasn't true. If they wanted to, they could have found me. They could have helped.

Someone still unknown to me must have paid the Hirsches living expenses in Belgium. I, and other girls as well, lived with the Hirsches and, of course, our upkeep was an expense for them. We also traveled, and all these expenses were paid by someone, perhaps Jewish welfare organizations. I believe my uncles and aunt gave as much as they could to these efforts. They were not well-off themselves. Despite a kind of uneasy feeling about how they had failed to help Stanisława over the years, I still regarded my uncles and aunt with great respect and visited them until the day they died. I hope and believe that I brought them a lot of joy.

These days I hear the stories of other people at conferences organized by the Hidden Children Organization, to which I belong—stories of how aunts and uncles and friends of deceased parents fetched their relatives or found ways to help them. My case was just a bit delayed, I suppose one might say, and indeed finally my uncles and aunt did wake up, remembered me, and made efforts to find me. Their interest in me and their ability to act upon it came as a result of the efforts of the American lawyer, Dr. Yaacov Griffel.

Dr. Griffel had a personal vision, a sense of urgent personal mission, to retrieve into the Jewish fold all of the Jewish souls—hidden children, mostly from Poland. If Dr. Griffel hadn't done this, I believe that I'd probably still be there, a person with a kind of double identity, living in a Catholic world perceived as somewhat hostile and feeling a Jewish identity, however vague and uncertain.

SHABBAT INVITATIONS

When I was in New York at the age of 19, religious families felt it a *mitzvah* (good deed) to host Jewish youth who had survived the war for Shabbat dinner, and I was invited to many homes. My uncles would have loved to have me with them every week, but I was invited out every Shabbat. Being new to the community made me a popular girl for matchmaking efforts.

My hosts, Moishe and Leah Katz, were my matchmakers and played a large part in sending me to Stern College, and I enjoyed their company. Bringing me to America was the joint effort of many people, and so I felt the need to be gracious and accept Shabbat invitations even if I didn't know what role my hosts had played in bringing me here. Most of the dinners were with much older people—their children were maybe a bit younger than I was. But I had fun. I went to synagogues with them, and they were looking for "matches" for me.

I spent Shabbat at some beautiful places. I have fond memories of Mr. Stein, a jovial grandfatherly type who hosted me and others from Poland for Shabbat dinners. He and his wife were big-hearted, easygoing people who opened their home to the Polish hidden children now living in the area.

America provided opportunities for finding a Jewish environment compatible with my eagerness to include more secular interests and ideas such as college education, equality of women, inclusiveness of viewpoints and lifestyles, community openness. In Antwerp, especially among the religious people, there was the expectation of a dowry. Many young men focused on learning Torah and hoped to find a bride whose parents could support them. Of course that left me out. I had arrived from a Catholic upbringing in Poland and was discovering Judaism, trying to experience life for the first time as a Jew. I wasn't thinking about marriage at all.

Even though I didn't have a dowry, they kept sending me on get-togethers with various young men, and so I went. I think I got a glimpse of the reality when, at a Shabbat dinner, a religious Jew in the diamond business casually remarked, "Who's going to marry you? You have nothing." Somehow that remark, hurtful as it may have seemed, strengthened my resolve to be more myself, and less what was expected of me. The absurdity, the futility, of meeting young men knowing that I would never be an appropriate marriage choice for them, freed me to be more independent. In Poland I had been popular with "boyfriends" galore. I was accepted in Poland, even though there was a kind of shadow over me because some people suspected I was somehow Jewish and not Catholic. But I was part of a group of young people and social relations were not difficult. The casual remark of a stranger who knew nothing about me, asking me sarcastically who would marry me since I had nothing, no dowry, was at once hurtful and a watershed in my life. After that incident, which had liberated me, I refused to date anyone in Belgium. I was free. What a relief!

I learned that in America it didn't matter if you had a dowry. But in New York I met no one that I cared for romantically. The few men that I met, who might have been prospects, weren't interested because communication was so difficult as I didn't speak English well. I went from feeling relieved that I didn't constantly have to meet eligible young men to feeling a sense of optimism and wonder about the unexpected variety of lifestyles in America. I was determined to succeed in America and I thought less and less about marriage and more and more about my personal future and succeeding in this new culture.

MRS. LEDERMAN

When the Ledermans came into my life, or I into their life, a change in my outlook evolved. They had just gotten married and they invited me to a Shabbat dinner. I was very excited about it because the husband spoke Polish. I had been introduced to this couple by Rebbetzen Davis, the principal of Beis Yaacov, the girls' seminary. She was a friend of Rabbi Lederman's wife and must have known that Rabbi Lederman spoke Polish.

Rabbi Lederman picked me up from Canarsie, Brooklyn, and took me to Borough Park. We arrived at their home, I met his wife, and was amazed that he spoke beautifully in Polish. By then my English was improving so I could communicate with his wife, and we shared stories about life in Poland and experiences of an immigrant in America.

The Ledermans invited me to spend Shabbat with them in the Catskill Mountains. The idea that there were mountain resorts for Jewish guests, Jewish culture, with kosher food, surrounded by forests and lakes was a revelation to me. The weekend was magical and time passed as if we were in a sort of fairytale setting where everything was new and beautiful to me. The most surprising revelation came after the magical weekend had passed and we were on the drive back home. Somehow, the subject of orphanages came up. I told them the story of how I had been in an orphanage in Poland as a child.

"Where in Poland was the orphanage you were you in?" Rabbi Lederman asked.

"In Bytom," I answered.

He was taken aback. "My mother was in charge of that one!" He smiled and waited for my response; perhaps I remembered her. I got shivers when I heard that Rabbi Lederman's mother was in charge of the orphanage where I had been taken, not quite willingly, by a kind of subterfuge. What a strange fate! How remarkable, how unlikely, that I ended up as the guest of my kidnapper's son! Years later I asked my mother if she remembered the woman's name from the orphanage. Sure enough, she told me it was a Mrs. Lederman. I knew how I felt about the orphanage—the sense of fear and betrayal—but I didn't know how to feel toward Mrs. Lederman. I started to remember my mother's story: how Mrs. Lederman came to the door and handed my mother $100, a lot of money at the time. She said to my mother, "Mrs. Łączkowska, this is for you to better yourself a little. Maybe with this money you won't have to work a double shift." It was suspicious, but my mother took the money. In my mother's mind at the time, Mrs. Lederman was wonderful, just trying to help us. But I believe that in Mrs. Lederman's mind, she was paying off my mother. The upshot was that she misrepresented her true intentions. She, as well as other people, felt my Polish mother had no right to raise me and that she could be paid off. This was monstrously untrue and cruelly inconsiderate. They were either incapable of seeing the truth of my mother Stanisława's profound love for me, her bravery in protecting me at the risk of her life and family, or they just didn't care. They did it in the name of God and never considered how my mother jeopardized her life, and the life of her family, to save mine. They wanted only to dismiss her, to get her out of the way so that they could "rescue" me.

Rabbi Lederman told me all kinds of stories about his mother. It turns out that Mrs. Lederman was a good friend of the wife of Władysław Gomułka, who later became the premier of Poland in 1966. In 1946, when I was in the orphanage, though he was not yet premier, he had a high rank in the Communist hierarchy. Gomułka's wife was Jewish but of course hid her identity.

Mrs. Lederman and Mrs. Gomułka were friends and together they helped Jewish people leave Poland. Gomułka helped Mrs. Lederman smuggle Jewish children out of Poland. I met Mrs. Lederman on a visit to Israel as an adult but the frailties of her age prevented us from having a meaningful conversation.

Decades after the war, after my time in the orphanage, Rabbi Lederman wrote to me, "I would like you and your husband to honor my mother for all the righteous deeds she did for children. I will bring her to you. She's a woman of valor." When I read the letter to my mother, she burst into tears. She looked at the pictures and recognized Mrs. Lederman. Mrs. Lederman was photographed wearing a wig, but my mother remembered her as younger, with braids wrapped around her head in the old-fashioned way. After looking at the pictures, my mother could not sleep for many nights.

She was hurt, as she remembered vividly the heartache of what she had experienced as my kidnapping, and she re-lived the frightening events in her mind. I thought to myself, "It is so unjust that Rabbi Lederman should ask me to honor his mother when it is truly my mother who risked her life and should be the one honored." My mother raised me, my mother suffered, and my mother jeopardized her life to save mine. Mrs. Lederman lured Jewish children away from righteous Christians, pretended to take them to an orphanage, and from my mother's perspective, paid for the children. My mother was catapulted into the past and could not stop going over and over the traumatic events in her mind.

I cannot call Mrs. Lederman a liar, because from her perspective, she did it in the name of God. And that is what most of the Jewish people I was surrounded by believed. I loved many of them, and although they tolerated me because I took to their religion, they weren't always sensitive to other people's feelings.

In the end, I wasn't disturbed by Rabbi Lederman's request. My mother received plenty of honors when she came to America. She was honored by *Sha'arit Ha'playta* (Hebrew: Surviving Remnants—a network of organizations providing community, resources, and support to Holocaust survivors), *B'nai Brith* (Hebrew: Children of the Covenant—a Jewish advocacy and community volunteer service organization), *B'nai David* synagogue, and other organizations. Many of my friends understood my mother's heroism; they opened their hearts and received her with open arms and admiration. At last she received the recognition she deserved for her bravery and her unwavering love and commitment.

As a personal footnote to history, so to speak, my mother Stanisława always had a bad feeling about that $100. She never converted the money to Polish złoty. It remained tucked away in a drawer for me, in case I needed it one day. She never used the money because she felt that using it would be like selling me. There was a great deal of trauma amongst the hidden children.

MEETING MANY RABBIS

After my arrival in America, there soon unfolded one of the most inspiring moments of my life. Ingrained in my soul forever is the astonishing experience of meeting the *Lubavitcher Rebbe*, Rabbi Menachem Mendel Schneerson. The meeting was arranged, based upon the miracle that a Polish Catholic girl who had grown up a Christian in a Christian Poland, was returning to her people, the Jewish people. I didn't realize that Rabbi Schneerson was the esteemed and beloved *Lubavitcher Rebbe* (rabbi). Being in his presence was like being in a space of light-filled energy. He sat across from me, at his

The Lubavitcher Rebbe Menachem Mendel Schneerson, early 1950s

desk. We spoke in Russian. He smiled and radiated a loving warmth, watching me intensely as I told him of my life adventures.

The *Rebbe* looked straight into my eyes, intensely, riveting me with the gaze of his piercing blue eyes, his holy energy isolating me from all else, including his assistants who stood by him. We talked about my life. Tears came into my eyes because the intensity of his interest drew from me details, memories, and feelings long buried, which now surfaced again: the pain, the confusion about my identity, the loss of my birth parents and brother, the loss of my Polish Catholic father who'd risked his life for me, my loneliness as I discovered more about my origins and withdrew from the Catholic world that had nurtured me. He listened. I felt that the Rebbe was almost a mind reader and that he understood me. Suddenly I was exhausted and could speak no more. The *Rebbe*, still sitting there as if he had endless time to listen to me, made me feel like I had spoken also for the millions who had perished, who could not ever speak to him. Then the *Rebbe* blessed me with a warmth that I had never experienced in another human being. Some of his blessings were mysterious, some straightforward—that I should have a good life and be a good Jew. At last, as I left, I could speak no more. My throat had closed, tears were in my eyes, and my life had somehow changed. I knew it, and I left the *Rebbe's* presence in silence, barely able to say, "Thank you," in a weak voice.

Rabbi Schneerson urged me to marry someone observant. He did not tell me to be religious. He said simply that if I married someone religious, I myself would remain religious. He just explained that it was important to marry an observant Jew.

CHAPTER SIX
FINDING FRED

In March, within a month of my arrival in America, my Aunt Hanka came to New York to meet me and she took me to her home in Detroit for a visit. It was there that I met a man who was different from all the others I had met previously. I met Fred Ferber. I was a religious Jewish girl when I visited my Aunt Hanka in Detroit but I

Fred Ferber, Detroit 1955

felt confused about Jewish observance.

While I was in Detroit, I went on a few "dates" but made no connection with any of the young men I met and, though all were fine people, I felt I couldn't get back home soon enough. There was one occasion that was different. It wasn't an uncomfortable "date" but instead, my aunt took me to a large B'nai Brith event. The president of the B'nai Brith told the crowd a somewhat sketchy story about me and how I was saved. Then, they handed me a guitar and asked me to sing. I went on stage and started to sing. I sang in Polish. Little did I understand how many Jews were repulsed by the Polish language which conjured up for them memories of the Holocaust. I sang away in Polish, oblivious to this reality. Amazingly, I got a lot of applause. Allowances had been made, I suppose.

As I was going off the stage, I noticed a young man, at a distance. He was far from me, but for some reason I looked across the crowd of faces and saw only his face. I didn't know who he was. He was talking to someone. The next morning, that young man I'd seen from afar, across a crowded hall, called me. He told me he had noticed me, that his name was Fred Ferber, he was also Polish (which was not unusual), and he hoped I'd like to see him. My mind went blank. I didn't answer and my throat felt constricted. I didn't understand why. Finally I squeezed out a reply, "Yes, sure."

When he picked me up for the first time, he wore a light gray jacket and he looked so awfully handsome to me. His smile seemed so natural, as if he smiled from within. He spoke softly, but somehow also firmly, as if he knew who he was and had no need to exaggerate; he fairly shone warmth and aroused interest in me. It was as if all his attention was on me, not on himself or anything around us. His radiance actually reminded me a little of the radiance of the *Lubavitcher Rebbe* and the *Rebbe's* words floated into my mind, "Marry someone religious."

We went off on our date and we talked and talked for hours, sometimes about matters of personal history, sometimes about our feelings and perceptions. We ate in Darby's, a fun restaurant and an experience I had never had. I realized that Fred did not keep kosher.

He ate a corned beef sandwich while I enjoyed a glass of tea. I kept remembering the *Rebbe's* words. And then, seeing Fred's smile, experiencing his warmth and his genuine concern for me as a unique person, which he somehow communicated by his smile, his questions, his attentiveness to me—seeing all this, and more, about Fred, it struck me. I suddenly realized that this man I had just met, after a couple of hours in his presence, radiated a warmth and sincerity which felt spiritual. Fred, I realized, was indeed a religious man, perhaps in his own way, whose love for others was genuine and was the essence of a religious soul.

Fred lived with his mother. They kept a kosher home but Fred ate in restaurants. Although at first this seemed odd to me, having been taught a stricter view, I came to understand Fred's Jewish observance. On our first date I ordered tea, just a cup of tea and nothing more. But I was so taken by Fred's presence and our sudden connection that I never noticed that I had missed dinner. I suppose I was the ultimate cheap date on our first evening together. I was enchanted, enthralled really. Fred spoke to me in Polish, shifting me back to a way of feeling and expressing myself that I hadn't experienced since leaving Sosnowiec. He affectionately commented on my Polish, which I guess sounded to him like a teenager's way of speaking rather than an adult's. He laughed with me, corrected my grammar here and there, made me feel we'd known each other forever. I was struck by his eloquent speaking style as much as by his profound ideas, all in Polish.

We had a world of experience in common. For the first time in America I was genuinely comfortable with a fellow on a "date." For the first time since leaving Poland here was someone who understood me as no one else did, understood my past, my childhood, the anguish of my separation from my mother. He understood.

During this first evening together, Fred told me that he had been in Mauthausen Concentration Camp, the camp in which my Polish father Jòsef had perished. It deeply moved me that despite the horrors he had experienced at Mauthausen Concentration Camp, Fred remained compassionate and hopeful. This quality of his character, which I so loved, had not been extinguished in the concentration camp.

Unlike others, Fred empathized with my struggle to reconcile my own feelings of loss. He understood how I missed my mother, understood my bond to my Polish family and love for them, and did not criticize me for those feelings. He never called my family *goyim* or devalued them as merely the ones who had saved my life. He talked about them just as I did—as my parents, my brother, and my sister. And he understood how badly I wanted to see them. It was, of course, impossible even to dream about bringing them to this country in 1962.

The more time I spent with Fred, the more I realized what an empathic, sensitive man I had found—someone who understood my past and, I realized, my soul. I was able to communicate to him and knew that he understood the deepest feelings I'd hid from others and always kept just to myself. I began to see that he was a man I could go through life with, who would be not only my lover, but also my friend. We became romantically attached and saw each other as often as we could. I had to go to school and return to New York, so Fred kept coming to New York for visits, and I would also travel to visit him in Detroit.

We shared many experiences, as if we were both awakening to aspects of life we had never cared for until being in each other's company. We explored Detroit together as Fred planned interesting excursions. A place that dazzled and enthralled us was Al Siegel's Elmwood Casino in Windsor, Ontario, across the river from Detroit, Michigan. The menu amused us with an array of dishes I had never imagined and couldn't eat, and an elaborate list of cocktails that seemed so very sophisticated to me, as if from movies I had seen. On another evening, we went to The Hungarian Village in Detroit and on the menu was a picture of a man and woman clad in folk costumes, dancing. *Dine and Dance. Hungarian Gypsy Music Every Night*, was printed on the cover. There followed a dizzying array of unique places Fred chose for us, all of which would be considered "historic" today.

It was as if Fred was determined to share with me every aspect of night life enjoyed in the Detroit area. And slowly it dawned on me. This was about more than just having fun or exploring Detroit. Fred was trying to put some distance between me and the pain of separation I felt, constantly feeling the loss of my parents—both sets of parents, and my brother and sister. We spent hours together and spoke about our lives, about our pasts, our joys, and our sorrows. In the beginning we recalled more of the sorrows, but as the months went by, as we learned about each other, the joys started to come through more and more. It was as if we gave each other permission to feel happiness again. We allowed each other to laugh again. And though the past held pain and sorrow, we granted ourselves the right to recollect happy memories. Gradually, we put the most painful episodes ever further behind us, having shared them and aired them. As we allowed ourselves to be distracted by the wonders of Detroit's varied haunts, just below the surface we were both healing, we were both reconciling the past with the present, and we were growing in our love for each other. When we were together, we allowed each other to be truly who we were, not who we pretended to be in polite company. When we were apart, we further deepened our bond in daily phone conversations.

And then, there were the flowers. So many flowers! How could any girl resist? How could I resist? Such beautiful flowers! Always different, always scented by nature and colored by God, I used to think. Fred showered me with flowers between our visits. He never let up. Every time flowers arrived, my heart leaped, my throat constricted, my eyes teared. Oh, to imagine someone loving me this much! Most especially someone who had met the real me, the girl who pined for her Polish Catholic family, who mourned the parents she never knew, who blamed herself for her Polish father's death because he had saved her! And all this seemed weightier than my guitar playing and my poetry. But nothing was too weighty for Fred. Fred loved every aspect of me just as I loved every aspect of him. The more I discovered of his remarkable tender soul, the more deeply I fell in love with him. Truth is, Fred and I are still falling in love with each other all these years later. And then there was, within me, the slow and steady accretion of Jewish knowledge, all in pursuit of my Jewish soul I sought to know, to understand, to express.

One visit to New York effectively summed up to me Fred's unique innocence and his self-assurance. In those days I was living with my religious Aunt Mania and Uncle Jack. We were sitting on her front porch when we were suddenly treated to the rather amusing spectacle of a fellow zipping down the block in a fancy Thunderbird convertible. "Aunt Mania, you have some racy neighbors I see." No sooner had these words crossed my lips when my jaw dropped. Oh no! It couldn't be. But it was. No stranger, this was my Fred, but how could this be? Words just failed me. Aunt Mania stared, wide-eyed and unbelieving. Fred's sudden surprise arrival on Shabbat at our home was shock enough. His emergence from a racy sportscar, hatless, a huge grin on his face, stunned us both. I just froze, thrilled to see the man I loved, amazed at his transformation to a playboy hotrodder, but feeling mortified that he had raced up in his rented Thunderbird on, of all days, a Saturday—the holy Shabbat. And not only did he have no hat on, but his hair was also flying in the wind like a teenage rock-and-roll star. I was thrilled and embarrassed all at once.

As far as she was concerned, my aunt sized him up pretty quickly. "How could I go out with a non-religious man?" she challenged me. It was true, I had to admit. Fred was not a strictly religious man, of course. But neither was he irreligious, if that makes sense. He respected religious practices, while living his life with a measure of joy and love, both of which became the cornerstone of my personal healing, just as his optimism had healed him after the war. Indeed, disrespectful he was not. Carefree would be a better description of him as a young man. Considerate of others' religious scruples, traditional, but not strictly observant. After all, he had suffered, and endured all he had seen in Mauthausen Concentration Camp; he could make his own decisions about life. And as I saw it, the most important decision Fred had made was to continue being the kind and considerate man he is, cherishing friends and helping others whenever asked. That is the man Fred still is, today more than ever.

Shocked by the sight of "Rock & Roll Fred," as she dubbed him, Aunt Mania carried on. But slowly her protests lost steam. Charmed by Fred's good-natured innocence, she quickly grew fond of him. By the time Shabbat ended, Aunt Mania was enjoying Fred's breezy and lighthearted affection. After Sabbat ended on Saturday after nightfall, late on a July night, Fred took me for a ride. Soon I too felt breezy and lighthearted in the Thunderbird as we drove out to Jamaica, Queens where Fred introduced me to his Aunt Cyla. It just so happened, purely by chance of course, that his entire family was there that weekend to meet me. Freddy and I laughed and laughed. And in the best of moods, looking at the twinkle in Fred's eyes, I met all his cousins. Fred planned and Fred surprised. We laughed, had fun, and overcame the past. Sometimes we laughed so hard that we cried, and when we cried from laughter, we cried a little for those we had lost, but we always sustained our joy and our love. And so it is today, for the past never disappears, but neither does love or the joy of life.

The next surprise Fred had in store for me was even bigger, more unexpected. Fred seemed to intuit that the best way to help me overcome my shyness was to surprise me, thrust me into situations unprepared and then be there for me, by my side, encouraging, smiling and holding my hand. The summer wore on. Our rendezvous continued. It wasn't a very hot summer, but it melded that year right into Indian summer—an early autumn warmth—and soon I found myself back in Detroit again. This time it was I who visited Fred and he made sure that we spent every spare moment together, which buoyed my spirit and deepened my trust in him. So in a way I should have been prepared when he suddenly announced, "Come on, I want you to see where my mother and I live." Up we went into a house. I had no idea whose house this was. He just opened the door. I walked in. And just that suddenly, I met Fred's mother.

We hugged, we smiled. As it turned out, no long introductions were needed. We looked at each other and energy flowed between us almost as if we already knew each other. I felt a strong sense of mutual recognition. I think Fred had prepared her, even though he had not prepared me. There was much we shared and many experiences that united us—the fact I had come to know Fred in a deeply emotional and spiritual way, knowing his past, helped establish a genuine rapport with his mom.

But there was something else, something quite astonishing, which took me by surprise and touched my heart. Fred's mother sat me down and explained to me that she knew my birth mother, she knew my family who had perished in the Holocaust, and she even knew my grandparents. I was startled by this sudden revelation and tears welled up in my eyes. And then the dam burst. So many emotions I had held back for all these years, so much I had kept hidden deep within myself, flooded into my consciousness. Fred's mother and my mother were from the same city. She told me how fine and loving and thoughtful my parents were, not just to compliment my birth family, but because this was the truth of my past. She even remembered how kind and thoughtful my grandparents had been!

Never had anyone described to me my mother and father in such a personal way. I cried and Fred's mother held me in her arms. I could not imagine such a coincidence. Was this a sign of some divine providence? Was this evidence of a higher connection between us? It couldn't be a mere coincidence that the man I had met across a roomful of people, as I remembered that first time I saw Fred, the man I was falling in love with—that his mother knew my mother and father, and even my grandparents. After I returned to New York, Fred's mother and I talked a lot on the phone. To this day I feel a divine providence in my meeting Fred, picking him out in a roomful of strangers, and falling in love with him.

THE RIGHT DECISION

Fred and I continued to deepen our relationship, continued to learn more and more about each other. Our courtship continued. It was a courtship strengthened by understanding each other's personal history, a courtship strengthened by our shared vision of a future uniting our souls in love, a true love imbued with hope and joy overcoming the sadness which had colored both of our pasts, in different ways.

July of 1962 came to New York City as a blistering heat wave. High temperatures in the 90s were a novelty to me and I thought about my mother Stanisława and my brother and sister in Poland who would be amazed at such a heatwave. I could not remember sweltering heat from my childhood in Sosnowiec. The heatwave caused people to unbutton shirts, fan themselves, and made New Yorkers feel they were somehow detached from everyday reality. It was just too hot to carry on as normal.

Then, without notice as usual, the man I loved, the one person who seemed to me to have peered into my soul and knew me as only I had known myself, arrived in the steamy city. Fred called me and we met as we usually did, but something was different. Still flashing his roguish smile, still radiating that optimism I had grown to depend on, Fred seemed different. It was clear that he had something on his mind. Now you might imagine it ought to have been obvious to me. But Fred waited until we were in a quiet place and then, in the record heatwave of New York City, Fred chose the moment and asked me to marry him. His eyes had a faraway look, as if he awaited guidance from above, even as he stared intently at me, and I looked at him. Suddenly I felt I was at that moment seeing the whole of Fred Ferber, heart and soul right there holding my hand. Time stood still. The world was just the two of us. Fred's quiet self-assurance and his profound certainty in our love, brought his proposal directly to my soul. I overcame the impulse to cry, an impulse welling up as a sense of vast relief and the deepest sense of joy I had ever felt; the world was balanced at last. I was alone no more. I squeezed out a whispered, "Yes!" But my leaping into his arms and kissing him was the answer he accepted. We loved each other more deeply and more honestly than I had ever imagined possible. We understood each other and our history.

I felt a certainty in marrying the stranger seen from across a crowded room, now my dearest Fred, my closest companion, my soul mate. And it went beyond just the two of us. I knew that Fred would be a wonderful husband and I also knew he would be a remarkable father. I had witnessed his close bond with his mother, I knew about the concentration camps, the deaths of his father and his brother there, the horrors he endured, and his hardships afterward. Though ours was a young relationship, it was founded on honesty and knowledge. And so, as the bustle of city life around us seemed suspended, as our lives clarified before us in the moment of commitment, we became engaged and set out upon our joint life path.

I asked Fred to come to a Shabbat so he could meet Leah and Moishe Katz. Moishe Katz had not met Fred before, but he knew Fred was in the electronics business and that he had a good business relationship with the Katz brothers, not only because he paid for merchandise on time, but because he was a pleasure to work with. They respected Fred on a personal level as well as in their business dealings.

PAPA AND ERNA MEET FRED

When I met Fred I was enthralled, and at the same time perplexed that this could happen to me. Across a room of strangers, I saw him. He too was a stranger. But he was also the one person who drew my unwavering gaze, and suddenly I think I blushed. I was staring. But at that moment I felt a spirit kindred to my own shining within him. Fred later admitted that he too was captured by me. But he was not unsure or puzzled, he was too self-confident for that. He had experienced enough of life, frightful and hopeful, to know his feeling was real. Over the months after our initial meeting, after we had come together, I believe by divine providence, and not by any introduction or mutual acquaintance, I came to know Fred and our love grew. We knew we were serious and so, I first told Fred who Papa Freilich and Erna were, and then called them and asked them to come from Belgium to New York to meet him. Their regard for me or their concern for me, I'm not sure which, won the day and soon they came. Papa was in the diamond business and traveled from Belgium to New York occasionally, so they just added an urgent trip to see me and assess Fred. They were intense, in their life style, and in their interest in my welfare. They wanted to meet the stranger from across a room, though I didn't explain our initial meeting quite that way. Papa was a smart man, and worldly, in his own unworldly way, if that makes sense. He was no pushover.

When Fred came to the house to meet Papa and Erna, Papa refused to come out to the living room. His mind was unsettled because he had concerns. Papa Freilich soon discovered that Fred wasn't strictly observant of the Sabbath, that he wasn't *shomer Shabbat* (Hebrew: Sabbath-observant), so he just dug in his heels and wouldn't come out to meet him.

Erna, on the other hand, had quickly made peace with Fred's level of religious observance and so she came out to meet him. She didn't judge him. Fred may have been a bit modern by their standards, but the force of his personal warmth, intelligence, and personal magnetism which have only grown stronger over the years, quickly won Erna over and they soon were chatting away happily like old friends. Erna and Fred even found a personal nugget of connection between them. In her youth, before she had met Papa, Erna had dated one of Fred's uncles. They laughed at this and at many other stories of the "old country" which they shared.

Finally, I went to get Papa and I insisted, "Listen, Papa, stop the games. You have two choices. Either go and meet Fred, or just sit here, and you'll never get to meet him again. And I will marry him anyway." Papa, hearing the warmth and laughter from the living room, knowing Erna had accepted Fred, relented and came in to meet him, a wry sort of smile on his face, almost as if by apology for his obstinate nature. And quickly, Papa warmed up. Papa deeply understood human nature, and his knowledge of the Torah kept him very sharp, but Fred is as brilliant a man as one might wish for, under any circumstances, and this was no different. Fred was already one step beyond Dale Carnegie in how to win friends and influence people, and soon counted Papa as one of his main allies in life. Papa and Fred understood each other and by evening's end viewed each other with newfound respect.

RABBINICAL BLESSINGS

Before we got engaged, I again was blessed to go to meet with the *Lubavitcher Rebbe*, Rabbi Schneerson. He kept me there for what felt like a long time. I explained to Rabbi Schneerson who Fred was, his experience in the concentration camps, and about my life experience, saved by righteous Christians. The *Rebbe* listened, intent upon every word I spoke, with deeper attention than anyone had ever accorded me. He blessed us both, though his blessing was not altogether within my ability to grasp. His blessing, I believe, was directed not only to us as individuals, but also to us as members of a people who had endured much and survived.

The *Rebbe* was unique among the rabbis I had met in that he put no pressure on me and asked nothing of me. He didn't say, as

Rabbi Menachem Mendel Shneerson

Papa Freilich sometimes did, "You must promise me this, or vow to do that." No. The *Rebbe* urged no promises, nor vows, nor commitments, but spoke directly to my soul in a way I cannot explain but has stayed with me as a kind of spiritual light within. In meeting the *Lubavitcher Rebbe* I felt a soul level commitment which transcended promises and vows and, most profoundly, seemed to come from my own soul. Instead of the *Rebbe's* voice, I heard in his presence an inner voice, an awareness, which had been almost stilled in my earlier life.

In Belgium, on Sunday nights, I would sit in a room near Papa while he spoke on the phone to someone named Moishe. I imagined this Moishe to be an old man with a long white beard. So when I met him and his wife Leah in Brooklyn, I was surprised to discover that they were only a few years older than I and had young children. They right away became my good friends and my Shabbat go-to family. There were four Katz brothers: Moishe, Sonny, Jake, and Yankel. I met them as a single girl just arrived from Poland with unknown prospects and a long road ahead of Jewish learning and social adjustment. So, when I met Fred, they were almost ecstatic in their enthusiasm. They, along with the Bunims and others, were excited that I had met a man who had apparently swept me off my feet—the stranger across a room, Fred. They were a close-knit clan and seemed so righteous to me that I nicknamed them "The Untouchables," after the famous Elliot Ness band of lawmen. They all lived in Far Rockaway, New York and were fortunate in their business ventures and, it seemed to me, in their personal lives as well.

On Sabbaths I always visited one Katz or another. They all felt committed to me, their own personal Polish rescue child, and to my welfare in America, and so they opened their hearts as well as their homes to me.

The Katzes were all in the electronics business, one way or another, and it turned out that Moishe already knew Fred from business. Fortunately, they all loved him and overlooked the fact that he was not a strict Sabbath observer. They wholeheartedly approved of Fred but nonetheless sought, in addition to the *Lubavitcher Rebbe's* blessing, the additional blessing of another famous rabbi, the *Skverer Rebbe*. Part of their motivation in seeking their *Rebbe's* approval was that they didn't want to take responsibility for my marrying a man who wasn't a religious Sabbath observer. That's it. They loved Fred and knew he'd be a perfect husband for me, but they wanted their *Rebbe's* blessing for their enthusiastic approval of the man in the sports car with the modern attitude toward life and observance. The Katzes thought it a big *mitzvah* to meet with various *Rebbes*. Papa Freilich pitched in too and arranged meetings with more than one *Rebbe*.

We went along with the succession of meetings with various rabbis and I felt sheltered by their blessings. Beyond the good wishes and the blessings of those who saw me as rescued from post-war Poland in the name of God, one reality was absolute for me. Accepted by the rabbis or not, I was determined to marry my one true love. Fred had asked me to marry him and nothing could or would stand in our way. And that was that. It felt good to give everybody the respect we knew they deserved. We felt our love was destined by God and our friends went along with the divine plan as we saw it.

OUR WEDDING

Erna and Papa Freilich were like my second parents, or I guess I should say they were like my third parents, though I never had any conscious memory of my birth parents. Because they were parental to me, I wanted my decision to marry Fred to include them just the same as I would have included my natural parents. They enthusiastically approved of Fred. One holdout, Sherman Gross, who had never met Fred, felt on principle that I should finish college and learn about the world before marrying. He felt I was too young and so he never showed up at our engagement party, our *Tannaim* (Hebrew: Conditions of Marriage; here, refers to an engagement party). Sherman was modern Orthodox so he naturally wanted me to marry a graduate of Yeshiva University. When Sherman at last met Fred at the wedding, he saw the reality of Fred—the amazing man that he

*Fred Ferber, Mira Łączkowska (Miriam Ferber),
Forest Hills, New York, 1962*

is, and his reservations about the man he had never met vanished.

The wedding and pre-wedding events passed like a dream before my eyes. Somehow, as marrying Fred transformed from my dream to my reality, I felt one step removed from the elaborate festivities which I believe is not an unusual experience for brides. For me, the past seemed to overlap the present, almost as a light mist intrudes on a summer day, arising from over a distant mountain. I remembered my birth parents, or imagined them, and the long winters with Stanisława, merging in my imagination. At the same time,

Before the chuppah. Erna Freilich, Mira Łączkowska (Miriam Ferber), Rose Ferber, Forest Hills, New York, 1962

Finding Fred

the pace of events accelerated around me. I saw myself circling Fred at the marriage canopy, heard words from Torah, focused on Fred's eyes shining love toward me, all as if in a dream—the past, present, and future suddenly vivid to me.

For the pre-wedding engagement party, the *Tannaim*, Rabbi Kreizwirth, now the Chief Rabbi of Antwerp, flew in. He was a close friend of Mr. and Mrs. Moishe Katz. Indeed, everybody I had hoped for came for the *Tannaim*, including Papa and Mrs. Freilich.

When Fred gave me the beautiful engagement ring he had chosen for me, I felt a flood of emotion. It wasn't just that I loved Fred and imagined a magical future together, it was also a feeling as if being lifted out of an unknown ocean onto dry land. Security, a new feeling, coursed through me as Fred put the ring on my finger. His eyes communicated to me his love and his happiness. The wedding was set for September 16, 1962, and when I look back at the photos of us standing under the marriage canopy, I see now what children we were, really, and not just me, but Fred also. I have never felt an intensity of emotion, a sense of time standing still, as I did on our wedding night. Surrounded by friends and family, I think we both felt as if there were only the two of us in the universe, all else just a dreamscape. I felt I was watching myself get married, watching Fred. I looked at this bride and groom as if I were floating above them. Even today, when I recall my wedding, I picture myself looking down at the bride and groom as if I were floating above them. Of course some people call this an "out-of-body" experience and so it was, I suppose, and so it still seems like that in my memory.

Mrs. Freilich and some of my other guardian angels planned the details of our wedding, and it was like nothing I had ever seen and certainly nothing I could have imagined. Amusingly, Fred's family were stunned and amazed that our wedding was so elaborate from the religious and ritual point of view. Not being strictly Orthodox, they had never seen such a religious wedding.

They must have thought I came from a different world as they looked on in amazement, but it was a happy amazement. Their love of Fred now encompassed me as they saw his joy mingle with mine. Of course, men sat separately and danced separately from women. One of the rabbis with whom I learned at Stern College, I believe his name was Rabbi Fulda, used to say that men and women dancing with others' husbands and wives was a desecration, and that made perfect sense to me.

The wedding was held at the Forest Hills New York Jewish Center. Fred wore a ceremonial white garment, a *kittel* (Hebrew: white garment worn at weddings and Yom Kippur), with a black overcoat. He wore a dark hat, in keeping with an Orthodox custom. I felt like a fairytale princess. I wore a flowing gown decorated with pearls which Mrs. Freilich had brought from Belgium. More than one dressmaker had worked on it, she told me. Mrs. Freilich also gave us many beautiful and unexpected gifts.

I have a picture at my wedding with Hershele Hirsch, Mala's son, on my lap. We're sitting at a table of New York *Rebbes*; all of

Right to left: Shari, Ronny and Annette Ferber, Michigan, 1968

them blessed us and I felt grateful and took their blessings seriously.

After the wedding, Fred and I moved to Detroit where he started a wholesale electronics company. He had founded "Ferber Television Service" which he gave to his mother who proved competent and capable of successfully running it. When they had first met, Papa Freilich made Fred promise he would close his business on Shabbat, and Fred did so without fail even though it was contrary to his business interests. We also promised to keep a kosher home, which we did. The rabbis who felt responsible for me as a hidden child returning to Judaism continually pressured Fred to be more observant and he certainly did his best. The new wholesale electronics business was closed on Shabbat just as he had promised Papa Freilich. Even though the retailers usually went to the wholesalers on Saturdays, Fred remained true to his word and never opened for that extra day of business, and the company was successful.

Miriam Ferber, Shari, Ronny, Annette Ferber, Michigan, 1969

I Was a Hidden Child

We had three wonderful children: Shari, Ronny, and Annette. To discuss them and our beautiful grandchildren would fill another memoir. Fred and I feel immensely blessed by our children.

HOMES

We purchased a corner house in Southfield, on Anna and Rutland, just behind B'nai David synagogue, where we became members. And we used to go to shul. We had a very traditional Shabbat. We never

Miriam Ferber and youngest child of Miriam and Fred, Annette, 1969

The Ferber family, Lake George, Albany, New York, circa 1972

went out and were always with family. We would go for services on Saturday, and then spend time with the children. But on Friday nights, no one ever left the house. We were always there with friends and family. Freddy's mom was always part of our Shabbat dinner.

The house in Southfield was very happy and full of children. It was only about 1,500 square feet, but everybody was happy there. We had a finished basement, and birthday parties were held there.

I Was a Hidden Child

Shari and Ronny Ferber, Southfield, Michigan, 1968

We didn't go to restaurants. And although we didn't have help, somehow we accommodated everybody, and it was a wonderful time.

In 1974, we moved to West Bloomfield. We lived in a white house on Far Ravine, and it sat on a very high hill. Even though

Ferber family, 1982

we had heaters under the driveway, it was very difficult to manage during the winter.

We had wonderful friends with young children in that neighborhood. The house was close to Hillel Day School, and it's where the kids spent their teenage years until they went to college. Our children kept in touch with the neighborhood kids from Southfield who would visit with us in West Bloomfield.

We had Shabbat dinner before Ronny's bar mitzvah in that house. Of course, I cooked! We had seventy or eighty people in the basement, and there was *gefilte* fish and chicken—a traditional

Shabbat dinner.

The house we live in now, on Upper Straits Lake in Orchard Lake, is our third house, and we moved here in 1988. We built it ourselves and love it.

FRIENDS

I like to keep in touch with my friends. I am in contact with most of my childhood friends from Poland and have acquired many wonderful American friends. I've remained in contact with my non-Jewish friends from elementary school. I went to my high school reunion a few years ago, in fact.

I had a lot of good friends, and I don't want to spend too much time listing them. I do have a childhood best friend, Romana Gruchała, or "Romcia." We lived in the same building. She was born with a hip problem—her leg wasn't attached correctly. The doctors operated on the wrong hip, and she's been crippled ever since. She was a very sweet child, full of life. She's still in constant pain but is always positive—we can really learn from her. Now her knees are giving her problems. But she perseveres and she lives in a beautiful

High school reunion (Miriam wearing pearl necklace in center), Sosnowiec, 1998

Mira's best frend, Romana Gruchała with Mira on the balcony, Sosnowiec, 1947

apartment with a telephone.

Aron and Hannah Weinstein were my neighbors in Southfield. Their son Bryan was the same age as Ronny, and they went to Hillel together. Mrs. Weinstein was a true *Yiddishe mama*. We would not drive on the high holidays. We would rest at her house between the prayers of Yom Kippur, and she hosted the breaking of the fast. She made packages for everybody and brought them to shul, so the minute the fast was over they could munch on her goodies. She's a wonderful lady, like a second mother to my son, and I

Romcia Gruchała, her sister Wanda Gruchała, Mirosława Łączkowska, Sosnowiec, 1947

Romcia Gruchała, West Bloomfield, Michigan, 1997

was like a second mother to Bryan.

Mrs. Weinstein was much older than I was, but we were good friends. Hannah and Aron were more contemporaries of Fred's mother. But the Weinsteins were always involved whenever we had a *simcha*. They always had wonderful dinners in their house, and our whole family was invited.

WANDA

Wanda's husband, my brother-in-law Janusz, died in a motorcycle crash at the age of 35 in 1955. Wanda was on the motorcycle with him, but only she survived; he was not wearing a helmet. After Janusz died and Wanda was injured but survived, she went into a state of shock, and I think also denial, and could not handle the loss, the emotions, the regret, the fear of being left a widow. Slowly she lost touch with everyday tasks and realities and started drinking to excess, and she became an alcoholic.

I'm in constant contact with my nieces, Wanda's daughters. After all, we're only a few years apart in age. After the fatal crash, my mother Stanisława took care of her daughter Wanda and Wanda's children for many years. Wanda died at the age of 56, and it was essentially my mother who raised her grandchildren.

It seemed an odd twist of fate that Wanda had pretended to run away from home to protect me with the invented story that she was my unwed mother and Stanisława was raising me in her absence. It was a story the Nazis accepted and this spared my life. After the motorcycle crash, Stanisława became the substitute parent for her daughter's children, once again, and once again bravely fulfilled the obligations of a loving and protective mother.

After the accident, times were tough and Wanda gave us a lot of problems. She and I drifted apart emotionally as she became a different person after she started to drink. First, she drank because she had lost her husband. Then she drank because her boyfriend was a drinker and threatened to leave her. In the end, she told him to leave, and then she drank herself to death. Neither Stanisława

Visiting the attic apartment, Jurek Łączkowski, Miriam Ferber, Sosnowiec, Poland, 1985

nor I could reach her anymore. The loss of Wanda was a terrible loss for my mother, for all of us. Wanda was a good woman, a brave protector of my life in her youth, a loving mother, all up until the fatal crash, before everything unraveled for her.

JUREK

My brother Jurek somehow married a dreadful, small minded, possessive and morbidly jealous woman. Of course, she had revealed little of her character before the marriage. But Jurek soon discovered that he'd married a woman who required a kind of special handling. My brother was no psychologist and did not know how to handle her. Jurek was a mining engineer who later began working for the Polish National Tax Authority. Jurek's wife was born and raised in a small village and was essentially uneducated. Sadly, she did not endeavor to rise to his level of education and so he went down to her level. I do not believe in the notion of a bad seed, but it is hard to avoid that description as she seemed perpetually mean-spirited, jealous, and malicious. She treated Jurek like an object, a possession. They never had children and they lived very poorly even though we tried to help by sending them money regularly. We later discovered that they kept the money under the mattress and never spent it.

One cannot blame them for their extreme frugality, of course; they were understandably afraid to spend money. In one sense, Jurek had a good life—he did not suffer financially, but his wife kept him away from everybody. When he was diagnosed with cancer of the saliva gland, she would not permit him to go to the proper doctors. He was weak and wouldn't fight back, accepting her irrational edicts. I wanted to bring him to the United States for surgery, but he wouldn't listen to me. We had found a surgeon here who wanted to operate on him and it should have been a minor surgery. But they neglected it, and he died in terrible pain, suffering unnecessarily. After refusing to allow him proper medical care, either in Poland or in the United States, his wife almost never visited him in the hospital; perhaps once or twice but only for a few minutes.

She seemed incapable of empathy, of considering anyone's suffering other than her own. Still, I try to keep in contact with her—cards on holidays, phoning to say hello. But as far as I can tell, she just has no interest in family, either in Poland or here.

GIVING

Miriam Ferber with Jurek Łączkowski, Sosnowiec, 1996

Finding Fred

In my lifetime, I have experienced giving and receiving, as most everyone has. What my birth mother Faygel gave me seems obvious, but is deeper than appearances, I believe. First, of course, she gave me life, my birth arriving during a time of crushing fear amid a world war. Next, she gave me seven months of constant care and protection against the backdrop of a cruel reality confronting my parents. My mother held me tightly in her arms for hours every day, I am sure of this. And at the last, she gave me life again, almost like a rebirth, from Miriam into Mirosława. Later in life, of course, I was able to give, and discovered that when you give, you experience a special feeling. When you receive, sometimes your feelings are mixed and ever since my teen years I've found receiving more challenging than giving.

I went to the funeral of Mrs. Rothbart, a religious woman my mother-in-law used to live with. A Yeshiva Beth Yehuda rabbi gave the eulogy. Though he spoke in English, not Yiddish, I felt annoyed because of his mumbling, perhaps due to his age. I said to myself, "Look, Miriam, you are at the funeral of Mrs. Rothbart, whom you knew for many, many years, and you better listen to what the rabbi has to say." So I listened. And he said something helpful and important to me. He said that Mrs. Rothbart was a charitable woman whose *tzedakah* (charitable giving) helped "repair the world." He reminded us that though it is fortunate to be on the side of giving, nevertheless, the one who receives is also fulfilling a Jewish precept, a *mitzvah*. Of course, the person in need allows the person privileged to help fulfill their role. You would not be able to give if another were not in need. And so I learned that when someone wants to give us something, we should not decline it. We should accept it, with gratitude, and say thank you.

I remember an event in my childhood of which my Polish mother Stanisława used to remind me. We were so poor, as many were after the war, and one day a beggar woman came to plead for alms. "*Proszę dać mi miłość.*" ("Please give me love.") I implored my mother, "*Mamusia*, give her something." My mother did not hesitate. Though we had no money in the house for the poor woman, my mother took a good nightgown she had and gave it to her. My mother often recalled this because in Polish there is a saying, "Give her the *koszulina* (nightgown)." And this time we really didn't have anything else to give her, so Stanisława literally gave the nightgown to her.

My mother told me when I was a young child that the most important aspect of giving is making sure the needy person feels no shame or embarrassment. We should give to others in a way that makes them feel good about it, which is not always easy.

Sometimes today I hear of poor women who have children, and then get married, and are desperate for funds. I tell my friends, "Let's give her whatever we can." And we each put some cash in an envelope and we give it to her. And that's that. She doesn't know who we are, doesn't feel obligated to us. There are many Jewish people who are poor and my mother-in-law believed in supporting widows. She donated money in Israel to widows.

RECOGNIZING HEROISM

In 1966, I brought my Polish mother Stanisława and my sister Wanda to America for the first time on an ocean liner of The Polish Ocean Lines called the MS Batory. It had been impossible to get them both to America for my wedding. So their first visit to us came twenty-one years after the end of the war, which seemed like a long time. Twenty-one years after the war I was unprepared for the angry reaction of many people I knew towards my mother and sister and I'll tell you why. Refugees from the European war experience, and carrying terrible memories, did not want any part of Polish people. More than two decades since the horrors of war, their anguish and anger surprised me. Even more surprising to me is that even today they are still so close-minded that they cannot recognize or acknowledge the reality of the many righteous Polish people who saved Jewish children. They don't realize how much these people jeopardized their lives to shelter Jewish children or the fear, hiding, loss and suffering they endured for the children. So I had a heck of

Left to right: Aunt Mania (Mączyk), Stanisława Łączkowka, Mira, Wanda Łączkowska, Jack Mączyk, New York, 1966

a time when my mother and sister came to visit us.

When my mother and my sister arrived, many people refused to receive them graciously or kindly. People could not believe how deeply attached to them I had become. They wouldn't understand the reality that I had lived in Poland for 19 years and that Stanisława and Wanda were the only family I knew, the only family I loved and kept in contact with. My mother and sister had risked their lives for me, my Polish father Józef had lost his life for me; they had all cherished and nurtured me. I cried my heart out and tried to explain that not all Polish people were the same. Some collaborated, either

Stanisława and Wanda Łączkowska aboard the Polish ship MS Stefan Batory en route to the US, 1966

willingly or under threat, but others did not, and instead braved disclosure and death to hide and protect Jewish children. These heroic Poles deserved recognition and respect. But I learned that you cannot convince people that someone is a hero by arguing about it. I was frustrated, distressed. I was young, naïve, inexperienced, and just couldn't bear the intolerance. That my Polish family was not graciously accepted caused me heartache and sadness.

Stanisława and Wanda stayed for three months. For three months I endured people making remarks, saying that I had "these *goyim*" (Hebrew: nations. In this case, a pejorative reference to non-Jews) in my house. The newcomers, greeners (Yiddish: newcomers) who had been through the concentration camps and survived, had witnessed Polish people at their worst. They had no room in their hearts for any positive association with Poles. Their pain, the terrors they had witnessed and endured, had made it impossible for them to distinguish between the actions of the Polish population who had collaborated with the Nazis and the many righteous Poles who had risked their lives to oppose the Nazis.

My first trip back to Poland was in 1967 when it was still a Communist country. It was a frightening time. It seemed to me that everybody here in America had the same critical words for me. "How can you go visit the *goyim*? The *goyim*!" they hollered. But despite all the screaming and scolding, I sorely missed my mother and my family. I left for Poland.

Warsaw's airport turned out to be just a tiny house with a fence. I think my visit had come just before the visit of Prime Minister De Gaulle of France who tried to turn Poland more to the west, away from Moscow's influence, but to no avail. The Soviet power was too great for Poland to oppose. On my flight to Warsaw there were only a few people on the plane. The Iron Curtain, as Winston Churchill had in 1946 described the Soviet lockdown of Eastern Europe, felt quite real to me as they interrogated me and searched my luggage. My mother, my brother, and Jerzy Gryt were all waiting for me and had started worrying as to why I wasn't coming out. I was struggling under the influence of terrifying ideas about the Communist Polish government which friends at home had planted in my mind before I had left. I felt fear welling up, and soon I was frantic. I knew Jerzy was waiting for me and would do whatever he could to protect me and it began to feel a little like the first time he had saved me from being kidnapped in the name of God. This time the threat was godless. At last I was permitted entry, released from questioning, and I saw myself, as if in a dream—it felt so unreal, rushing toward my family who had been getting more worried by the moment.

I stayed in Poland for only a week. A short week, but a long week if you measure it by all the emotions and memories that filled it. Mostly I felt a sense of joy, a sense of returning to my childhood, but without the bad memories. All the sights, sounds, the language, the food, even the familiar smells of home, of childhood, felt magical to me, shifted me into the past in my mind. When I left after a week, I felt I had had my "fix." I had sorely missed my family, deeply needed to see them, and after one week I had done so, with many happy and new memories of Poland, the country of my childhood and youth.

FINDING COMMUNITY

In 1991, I went to the first international gathering of child survivors. 1,800 people showed up at the first "Conference of the Hidden Children." Imagine! Many countries around the world have their own chapters, and many states in the United States have their own. I also go to the conferences which convene in different states and countries annually. We are like an extended family filled with love and understanding for each other. We cry together sometimes, we sing together often, and we dance together at the drop of a handkerchief, so to speak. Many of the attendees speak of their misfortune, then and now. I understand their feelings, I know what they had suffered. For many, the past lingers within them. It is sad to see that some continue to view life in a regretful way.

    I have not found the key to unlock the past for others. But the love I have with Fred and my trust in him has helped make the difference in my life. I also understand the importance of forgiveness to many who went through the war. But then, who am I to grant forgiveness? The past is of course gone and I believe that only God can decide who or what is forgiven.

    Before the Hidden Children Foundation existed, none of us could even talk about the fact that we were hidden. You see, one aspect is the guilt we felt over having survived while others were tortured, murdered, nearly murdered, left for dead. Many felt that the concentration camp survivors thought that we hadn't gone through as much they had. It is difficult or impossible to discuss such things really. Some hidden children who had never been in the camps felt they hadn't gone through as much as others had. But hidden children of course suffered and came away with unshakable memories, and grief.

    Most hurtful to me was when I experienced that my Polish Catholic family was not treated right. So when I invited my mother again (this time with her son Jurek) to my son's *bar mitzvah*, I admonished my family and my in-law's and friends. I told them if they made one wrong move, I would never speak to them again. So all of a sudden, they were nice to my mother. Of course, *Sha'arit*

Ha'playtah honored them. The synagogue president happened to be a Polish Jew and he understood and welcomed them, so they received the respect they deserved.

VISITING POLAND

I never really cared for what people said about returning to Poland

My first trip back to Poland. Stanisława Łączkowska, Jurek Łączkowski, Hania, Miriam Ferber, Warsaw, Poland, 1967

I Was a Hidden Child

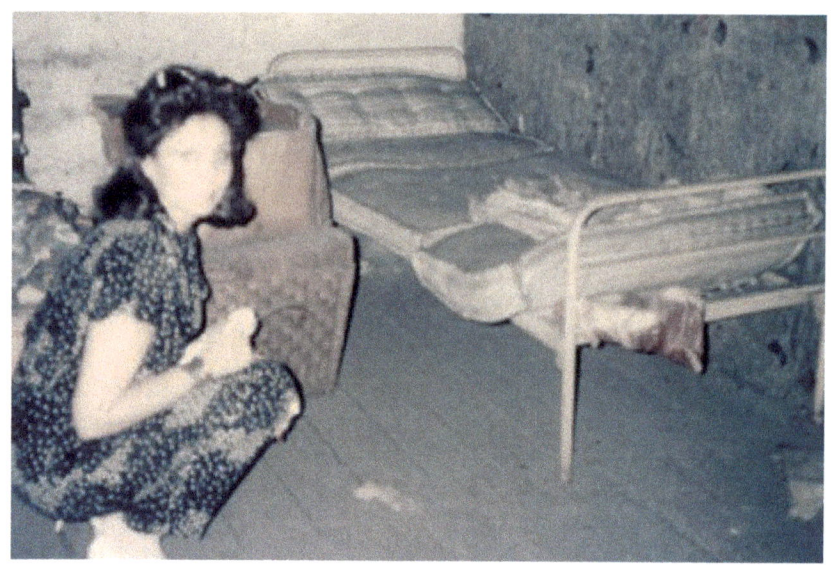

My bed in the attic apartment. Miriam Ferber, Sosnowiec, 1985

after the war. There was a stigma about Jews visiting Poland, but I went back to see my family whenever I could, and Fred would go with me. Whenever we could get a visa, I always visited my family. I was criticized every time. Only recently have survivors returned to reconcile their past and teach their loved ones about their heritage.

Many fail to understand that this is the family that raised me. This is the family I know. This is the family I love. And when I go there, I'm one of them. They know that I am Jewish. Maybe I have an identity crisis in my heart sometimes. When Christmas comes, maybe I like the Christmas tree and I like the decorations and so on; but, believe me, I know exactly in my head who I am, and now I am thrilled that I am who I am.

Jerzy Gryt, the UB guy who rescued me on the border, passed away in 2010. My sister Wanda died in 1980. My mother Stanisława in 1983. And my brother Jurek in 2001. Wanda's children are still alive. They are only about two or three years younger than me. Fred and I go to Poland often to visit my family, and my friends, and some of them come to visit us here.

Visiting the attic apartment. Shari Ferber, Annette Ferber, Jurek Łączkowski, Miriam Ferber, Fred Ferber, Sosnowiec, 1985

DREAMING OF MY BIRTH PARENTS

I have no memory of my birth parents, and the only pictures I have of them I received much later on, when I came to America. But I think of my birth mother much more now than I did before. I loved my Polish mother, and she was the only mother I knew. But sometimes she would say to me, "What kind of a mother leaves a child?" Perhaps she was angry; she wasn't always sure of herself.

Only after I became a mother myself, and a grandmother, could I understand what it meant for my birth mother to give me up. I think it was easier for her to hold her son in her arms and go into the crematorium than to give away a child.

When I think of my birth mother, she is always some place in a fog. I did not see her picture until I came to this country and met my uncles. But the first time they showed me her picture, I knew she was my mother. I do resemble her, and I have some of my father's features. And I also look like my brother Leo.

My mother has never come into my dreams. I think about her, but I don't feel a closeness to her. It's like somebody showing you a picture and saying, "This is your uncle. He was handsome. He is not alive any more." You might think, "Okay, it's my uncle." But it would be hard to feel close to him. My birth father, Shlomo Mączyk, appears in a fog the same way my mother does. The only connections I had to him were his two brothers and sister.

It was always my Polish mother whom I cared for and worried about. She adopted me when she was 45 years old. She was overweight and I was always afraid she would die of a heart attack. I slept with her in the same bed and always held her close to me. I'd wrap her arm around me and listen to her breathe. I would hear her heart. She was the only mother I knew.

I was three years old when my Polish father, Józef Łączkowski, died in Mauthausen. I don't remember him, either; it's also foggy. I do remember his presence in our home. But I never knew him as part of my life. I only remember my mother lifting me to see him through the peephole when we were in jail. But he has come into my dreams many times. I don't know why.

Maybe I dreamed about him because I was the Jewish child in their house. I feel like he died because of me, even though after the interrogation in jail they told him he would be released. It was so close to the end of the war that they didn't care any more whom they killed; not that they cared about whom they killed in the first place. They just sent him away to Mauthausen, and he died of typhoid fever. He was not executed; his death was from typhoid which was epidemic in concentration camps, labor camps, and, earlier on, in crowded ghettos. I always feel like my Polish Catholic family, who spared nothing to protect me, went through all of that trauma because of me. My Polish mother lost her husband because of me. My Polish sister was forced to flee and go into hiding because of me. Their lives were turned upside down. As time goes by, I appreciate their love for me more and more.

THE BRACELET

My birth mother gave my Polish mother a gold bracelet when she came to visit me for the last time. When I found out I was Jewish, my Polish mother said I should take it because she wanted me to have a connection to my Jewish mother. But I didn't take it. And then when she came to visit me, she again brought the bracelet, and I said, "No, *Mamusia*, you keep it." In 1966, she again brought it. I went to a jeweler and I bought her a charm and wrote a message to her on it. And then she lost the bracelet in Poland, and she was sick with remorse! She offered a reward for its return, but it was never found.

I should have kept my birth mother's bracelet when *Mamusia* gave it to me. Oh, how I wish I had! But that was when I didn't feel sentimental for my birth mother's things. Now that I'm older, I would love to have her bracelet. When I was young, 22 or 23, I was ignorant and didn't think about it. I wanted my Polish mother to have it, and I didn't want her to have any thoughts that I was taking away something my birth mother had given her. I wanted Stanisława to know that she was my mother.

CHURCH AND WISE MEN

I love churches and just being in a church. And I still go to church whenever I am away. I always go to church and light candles for my

My birthday party in Sosnowiec. Waldek, Miriam Ferber, 1985

departed family. But no priests, no mass. I just go from one place to another. I see all the idols. I don't pray, but I'm comfortable in a church and can sit there peacefully.

Kraków has a famous church and when I sit there, I feel good. During Christmas, I'd go to church in a second, even just to see the decorations.

I had an audience with the pope in 1985. We went to Poland with our children. At that time, none of them were married. A friend had arranged an audience for us. Of course, I was thrilled. The pope came and I kissed his hand, and in proper Polish I said, "Our dear father, may God bless you and keep you in health and happiness." I think I said all the right things. And he asked me, in Polish, where I was from. So, I said, "Sosnowiec." He was from Wadowice, which is very close to Sosnowiec.

The pope looked at me and asked, "Where are you from now?" I was wearing a white suit, different from all the others. The women around me were wearing scarves on their heads. I had none. I told the pope, "I am from America." I gave him a piece of paper. It

Shari, Annette, Fred, Miriam Ferber, Pope John Paul II, Rome, 1985

was a prayer request, and I had listed four names. He opened it and saw the four names: Faygel Zeilender, Shlomo Mączyk, Stanisława Łączkowska, and Józef Łączkowski. The Pope looked at me and he looked at the names. And he said, "*Rozumiem*," (I understand).

There will never be a pope like John Paul II again. He was one of a kind. When he was younger, he used to play soccer in Kraków with Freddie's uncles. I don't know how our friend got us an audience with him; probably an appeal to his past, and to the war and its effect upon the Jewish people for whom Pope John Paul II had genuine empathy and understanding.

YIZKOR

When it comes to *yizkor* (Hebrew: Community-wide memorial service for the departed), to remembering the departed in my family, I always pray for two fathers, two mothers, two brothers, and one sister. I light *yahrzeit* (Yiddish: candles lit on the anniversary of a family member's passing) candles, commemorating the anniversary of their passing, I do that for both of my sets of parents. When I pray for my mother, I have two mothers. And so it will always be, as long as I live to do so.

I had a whole to-do when my brother Jurek died in 2001. He died on a Monday, and the funeral was on Thursday. On Friday night, I went to Kraków to the Remuh synagogue (which is 600 years old), and I wanted to light a *yahrzeit* candle for him. Most of the people in that synagogue are remnants of the Jewish people in Poland and don't even know for sure if they themselves are Jewish. But they call themselves Jewish. The people at that synagogue didn't want me to light a candle for my brother Jurek. They wouldn't allow it because, as they told me as a rebuke, "He was a *goy*." And just like that, once again I had to deal with the same emotions I had when my mother came to Detroit. I was so frustrated and upset.

Among all these people there was a young *Lubavitcher* who was about 18-years-old. I went to him and said, "You've got to help me. You've got to find me a candle, whether they want it or not, before Shabbat." I told him that I knew Rabbi Shemtov in Detroit and that I needed help. I asked him, "What are you doing here? I thought Rabbi Schneerson didn't want any *Lubavitchers* on the ground in Poland." He explained that they were there for a different reason, to educate Jewish travelers. He helped me out and got me a candle. He told me to light it, even to say *kaddish* (prayer for the dead) for my brother. I had to fight for it, but this *Lubavitcher* was there. They always come through, the emissaries of the *Lubavitcher Rebbe*, Rabbi Schneerson. The compassion, the understanding, the resourcefulness of these people is unbelievable.

FINAL COMMUNION

I started going to Poland by myself almost every year beginning in 1967. Fred went with me for the first time in 1972, and we returned together about three times before 1985, which was when we took our

Miriam Ferber, Stanisława Łączkowska, Fred Ferber, Zarki, Poland, 1982

children for the first time. I always went to Sosnowiec; that's where my family was. But it was hard to get visas.

In 1973, I went to Poland by myself. It was October because I came for All Saints Day, which is on November 1st. It was almost winter, and my mother was chopping wood she could use to make a fire to keep warm. As much as I felt sentimental toward the apartment because I was raised there, I sat down with her and said, "You know, *Mamusia*, we have to forget sentimentality. I would love to see you in a modern apartment with heating and a bathroom."

Though at first my mother Stanisława resisted the idea of moving, eventually she said okay; she agreed to what I thought best for her. I bought her an elaborate apartment by Polish standards, thinking this would make her happy. And yet, it didn't make her happy, as I had hoped. She liked the building, even enjoyed showing it to her friends, but she continuously reminisced about the old attic

Miriam Ferber, Stanisława Łączkowska, Zarki, Poland, 1982

apartment. I wondered why, after all of our costly efforts, Stanisława longed for that attic. But we furnished the apartment and gave her all the luxuries. My dear, dear mother, my brave tigress, my savior, my constant and ever devoted protector, Stanisława Łączkowska, lived there for ten years, until her death in 1983.

My mother Stanisława became sick in 1980. I brought her to Detroit for three months shortly after my sister had died. She came with her granddaughter Basia, and I could already see signs of her aging. She went back to Poland and had an accident. She fell. From then on, Stanisława went downhill and I was in Poland just about every six months. Watching her helpless—someone who had been so self-sufficient, so sharp, and so brave—was very painful. She was later placed in a hospital and she quickly worsened. Confinement to a hospital ward, feeling helpless, losing touch with everything important, everything familiar, did not agree with my mother. Soon, she didn't recognize us. The tigress who had protected me against all challenges

Miriam Ferber, Stanisława Łączkowska, Sosnowiec 1983

was now rapidly failing. The end came quickly, inescapably, and sadly. *Mamusia*, my smart, independent-minded and courageous mother, Stanisława, died quietly and isolated from all she had known through her lifetime, at the age of 83 in Sosnowiec, Poland.

I cried my heart out at the funeral. It was during martial law in Poland and the priest feared even to talk about how, against all odds, Stanisława had saved my life. Saving Jewish lives was still a taboo subject in Soviet-controlled Poland. And so, the priest simply made note to the mourners that, "Mrs. Łączkowska had many secrets. And she took those secrets to the grave." But the priest wasn't successful in hiding the truth, not telling the story, for, in fact, by then, so long after the war, everyone already knew what she had done for me.

It was a big funeral, in large part because so many people wanted to see if I would take the communion or not. Would a Jewish woman, raised as a Catholic through her teenage years, saved by a Catholic family, would she? We have to see for ourselves. Well, they did see. Yes, I did take the communion. I took the communion for my brave

My mother and Wanda with my two older children in 1966

Mamusia who had sacrificed and risked so much for my welfare, for so many years. I took it because I felt sure this was what my mother would have wanted. It was vitally important to me to honor my mother. And to me, it was just a little wafer. So I told myself. I am glad I did this for Stanisława.

I took communion with my brother, who also never went to church. He was married to a woman who was divorced, so he couldn't be part of the Catholic religion anyway. But we did not go to confession, and this is a very big sin in the Catholic religion.

We buried my mother with all kinds of honors. Over the years, she had saved money to build herself an elaborate, marble tombstone. I was very upset about this because she had built it while she was alive. Once, when Fred and I went to Mauthausen-Gusen, we took some of the earth from Mauthausen, which was where my Polish father had died. We placed that earth in my mother's casket. My mother included my Polish father's name on the tombstone, though it is symbolic.

Fred with my mother Stanisława and my brother Jurek, Zarki, Poland, 1982

Now Mamusia is there with my brother and sister.
I think of them all the time.
Life does deal sorrows. But life also deals joys.
I believe we can celebrate the joys though we remember the sorrows.
My joy in life is my family, Fred, our children, our grandchildren.
I hope as you have read my story that you have focused on your own joy. And, though we may never meet, I wish you blessings, as others wished me blessings. That seems to work. I hope it works for you.
Thank you.

Miroslawa Łączkowska, now Miriam Ferber, and Fred

FAMILY AND FRIENDS' ALBUM

Fred, Miriam and Dzidek, Kraków

American friends at my 75th birthday party, 2017

Polish family and friends, Sosnowiec, 2017

I Was a Hidden Child

My son Ronny and Rabbi Kreizwirth, West Bloomfield, Michigan

Miriam with Rabbi Chaim Kreizwirth

Family and Friends' Album

Fred's 90th birthday, children and grandchildren of Miriam and Fred, 2019

Wth my friend Grażyna Rezner, 1980, West Bloomfield

With my nieces and nephew: Jacek, Basia, Miriam and Hania, Sosnowiec

Moishe Katz and my son Ronny

Family and Friends' Album

Shari and Papa Freilich, B'nai Brak, Israel

Shari, Miriam and Annette Ferber, 1998

Rabbi Chain Kreizwirth, my mentor

Family and Friends' Album

Rabbi Chain Kreizwirth, my mentor

Fred and Miriam with her mother-in-law

Moishe Katz, Fred and Miriam

Family and Friends' Album

With friends

Miriam with Rabbi Kreizwirth and his wife Sara, Brooklyn, New York, 1980

Rabbi and Mala Hirsch, and Miriam

Miriam and Rabbetzen Sara Kreizwirth

Hania, Miriam and Halina, Sosnowiec, 2016

I Was a Hidden Child

*The graves of my Polish family who saved my life—
the Łączkowskis*

Visiting the graves of Sara and Rabbi Chaim Kreizwirth

Visiting the graves of Erna and Papa Freilich, 2019

Miriam and Fred

Family and Friends' Album

Miriam and Fred

Miriam with Romana, Sosnowiec

Family and Friends' Album

Miriam and Fred, Florida, 2022

Guardian angels of my mother Stanislawa who took care of her during my absence

Miriam and Fred

Family and Friends' Album

Miram in, Brooklyn, New York, 1962

Our family with Uncle Herman and Mother Rose, 1986

On the opposite page:
Leo and his parents were from Sosnowiec, Poland. In spring of 1943 the Jews were moved to a ghetto in the Środula suburb, where his father was murdered. Leo and his mother and most of the other Jews from the area were deported to Auschwitz. His sister Miriam was adopted by a Polish family and survived.

Family and Friends' Album

www.ingramcontent.com/pod-product-compliance
Lightning Source LLC
Chambersburg PA
CBHW061413090426
42742CB00023B/3459